THE MEANING C

YVES CONGAR, O.P.

THE MEANING
OF
TRADITION

Translated from the French by A. N. Woodrow

With a Foreword by
Avery Cardinal Dulles, S.J.

IGNATIUS PRESS   SAN FRANCISCO

Original French edition: *La Tradition et la vie de l'Église*
Éditions du Cerf, Paris

Original English edition
© 1964 by Hawthorn Books, New York
All rights reserved
Published with ecclesiastical approval

Cover art:
Pentecost. Enamel from the Verdun alterpiece. 12th c. (detail)

Nicolas of Verdun (c. 1150–1205)
Sammlungen des Stiftes, Klosterneuburg Abbey, Austria
© Erich Lessing/Art Resource, New York

Cover design by Roxanne Mei Lum

Published in 2004 by Ignatius Press, San Francisco
This edition published by permission of Éditions du Cerf, Paris
Foreword © 2004 by Ignatius Press
ISBN 978-1-58617-021-9
Library of Congress Control Number 2004103527
Printed in the United States of America ∞

CONTENTS

FOREWORD

As the twentieth century recedes into history, the profiles of its theological giants loom ever larger. Yves Congar was one of those giants. Born at Sedan in 1904, he became a seminarian in Paris in 1921, entered the Dominican novitiate in 1925 and received priestly orders in 1930. In 1937 he published *Chrétiens désunis*, a study of the ecumenical movement, as the first volume of a series that he himself edited: Unam Sanctam. In the following two decades, he became chiefly known for his work on ecclesiology. Regarded in some circles as a dangerous innovator, he was treated with suspicion and had to endure suspension from teaching and occasional banishment from France during the 1950s.

In 1959 Pope John XXIII restored Congar's good name by appointing him a theological consultant to the preparatory commission for the Second Vatican Council. At the Council itself, Congar's influence was equal to, and perhaps greater than, that of any other Catholic theologian. His influence is manifest in the Council's teaching on Revelation, on the Church, on the laity, on ecumenism, on missiology and on many other topics.

After the Council, Congar's health was affected by a degenerative sclerosis, but he remained extremely productive almost until his death in 1995. His last major work was a three-volume study of the Holy Spirit. In recognition of his achievements, Pope John Paul II made him a cardinal in 1994.

While working for the Council, Congar collaborated in the study on "Tradition and Traditions" conducted under the auspices of the Faith and Order Commission of the World Council of Churches. In 1960 and 1963 he published the two volumes of his *Tradition and Traditions*, which many consider to be his most important publication.

The Second Vatican Council set forth the Catholic doctrine of tradition in the second chapter of its Constitution on Divine Revelation. That chapter stands among the principal accomplishments of the Council. Robert Imbelli once wrote: "Were I asked to state briefly the major theological achievement of the Second Vatican Council, I would unhesitatingly reply: the recovery of *tradition*." [1] And, as Joseph Ratzinger has observed, it is "not difficult ... to recognize the pen of Y. Congar" in the ideas and language of the text. [2]

Four centuries earlier, the Council of Trent had formulated the Catholic theology of tradition in opposition to the Protestant idea of "Scripture alone". In upholding irreversible apostolic traditions, the authors of that decree evidently had in mind beliefs such as the perpetual virginity of Mary and practices such as infant baptism and the sign of the cross, which were not attested in Scripture but seemed to go back to the very beginnings of Christianity. Catholic theologians in the post-Tridentine period came to view tradition as a second source, parallel to Scripture, transmitting truths explicitly revealed to the apostles but not consigned to writing in the canonical Scriptures.

This concept of tradition, however, was not adequate to deal with dogmas such as the Immaculate Conception, which emerged as a popular Catholic belief only in the second

---

[1] Robert P. Imbelli, "Vatican II—Twenty Years Later", *Commonweal* 109 (October 8, 1982): 78.

[2] Joseph Ratzinger, "Commentary on *Dei Verbum*", chap. 2, in *Commentary on the Documents of Vatican II*, ed. Herbert Vorgrimler (New York: Herder and Herder, 1969), 3:184.

millennium and was first defined as Catholic dogma in 1854. Some Catholic theologians, perceiving this insufficiency in the accepted Catholic theology of tradition, began to grope for a more open and dynamic concept.

Carrying the new tendency to an extreme, the Modernists devised an evolutionary theory of doctrine in which tradition functioned as a principle of transformation. But in this theory Christ became a mere point of departure for a revelatory process that went far beyond him and the apostles. Not surprisingly, Modernism was condemned as a heresy.

At the beginning of the twentieth century, Maurice Blondel sought to carve out a middle path between post-Tridentine and Modernist theories of tradition. The true theory, he maintained, should be neither pure flux nor static permanence, neither Procrustean nor Protean, neither "veterist" nor modernist. To his lasting credit, he rediscovered the capacity of tradition to transmit what was already known in an implicit way but not yet formulated in conceptual terms.

Yves Congar revisited the whole problem of tradition in the light of his vast knowledge of the Church Fathers, the medieval Doctors and modern ecumenical literature. While standing in the footsteps of Blondel, he greatly enriches the theological dimensions.

For Congar, tradition is a real, living self-communication of God. Its content is the whole Christian reality disclosed in Jesus Christ, including the implicit contents of that disclosure. The Holy Spirit is the transcendent subject of tradition; the whole Church is its bearer. Thus tradition is an essentially social and ecclesial reality; its locus is the Church as a communion. It is transmitted not only by written and spoken words but equally by prayer, sacramental worship and participation in the Church's life. Tradition, while consisting primarily in the process of transmission, is not sheer process.

Its content is expressed to a greater or lesser degree in a variety of documents and other "monuments", as Congar calls them. Interacting with the consciousness of those who receive it, tradition develops and is enriched in the course of centuries. Continual meditation on the inspired Scriptures on the part of those who obey the Gospel gives rise to new insights as to what was tacitly communicated in the original Revelation. The Church's teaching office, or Magisterium, has the commission to supervise the process of transmission, to stigmatize errors and to define revealed truths as they become clear to the believing Church.

These and similar ideas, developed at length in Congar's masterly two-volume work, are concisely summarized in the present volume, *The Meaning of Tradition*. Published shortly after the completion of the two-volume work, it is more orderly and concise and preferable as an introduction to the theme. The earlier work can profitably be consulted to fill in the historical background and explain the debated questions.

When I have taught material on tradition to seminarians and graduate students, I have regularly used this book as my primary text. But, being out of print, the book has been difficult to obtain. The present reprint will be welcomed by many who turn to Congar as perhaps the greatest master of the theology of tradition who has ever lived.

Avery Cardinal Dulles, S.J.
Fordham University, New York City

INTRODUCTION

The following story was told to me by an Anglican friend. He was a member of the delegation sent to Moscow in August 1956 to establish theological relations between the Anglican and Orthodox Churches. During the discussion the question of tradition and its relationship with Scripture was raised. The Russian interpreter, doubtless unacquainted with ecclesiastical terminology, spontaneously translated the word "tradition" by the expression "ancient customs".

Many people, and possibly some of the readers of this little book, may have the same idea of tradition as did the Russian translator. For many, tradition is simply a collection of time-honored customs, accepted, not on critical grounds, but merely because things have always been so, because "it has always been done". Any attempt at innovation is opposed in the name of tradition, which is considered first and foremost as a conservative force in society, and a safeguard against a dangerous liking for novelty, or even against any suggestion of a wider outlook. Tradition is favored because it prevents change.

We speak of the traditions of a school or of an organization: the traditions of Oxford or Harvard, of the army or navy, and equally of the different religious Orders or simply of certain families. We speak of national or regional traditions. In these examples the word "tradition" connotes something more than mere conservatism; something deeper is involved, namely, the continual presence of a spirit and of a moral attitude, the continuity of an *ethos*. We might even say that just as rites are the expression of a profound religious reality, so these traditions, which enshrine and safeguard a certain spirit, should comprise external forms and customs in such perfect harmony with this spirit that they mold it, surround it, embody and clothe it, so to speak, without stifling its natural spontaneity or checking its innate strength and freedom.

These traditions lead us to suspect that tradition is not just a conservative force, but rather a principle that ensures the continuity and identity of the same attitude through successive generations. A sociologist defined it accurately: "Tradition, in the true sense of the word, implies a spontaneous assimilation of the past in understanding the present, without a break in the continuity of a society's life, and without considering the past as outmoded." [1] In its different forms, tradition is like the conscience of a group or the principle of identity that links one generation with another; it enables them to remain the same human race and the same peoples as they go forward throughout history, which transforms all things.

Paul Claudel compared tradition with a man walking. In order to move forward he must push off from the ground, with one foot raised and the other on the ground; if he kept both feet on the ground or lifted both in the air, he would be unable to advance. If tradition is a continuity that goes beyond conservatism, it is also a movement and a progress that goes beyond mere continuity, but only on condition that, going beyond conservation for its own sake, it includes and preserves the positive values gained, to allow a progress that is not simply a repetition of the past. Tradition is memory, and memory enriches experience. If we remembered

---

[1] M. Dufrenne, "Note sur la tradition", in *Cahiers Internat. de Sociologie* (1947), p. 167.

nothing it would be impossible to advance; the same would be true if we were bound to a slavish imitation of the past. True tradition is not servility but fidelity.

This is clear enough in the field of art. Tradition conceived as the handing down of set formulas and the enforced and servile imitation of models learned in the classroom would lead to sterility; even if there were an abundant output of works of art, they would be stillborn. Tradition always implies learning from others, but the academic type of docility and imitation is not the only one possible: there is also the will to learn from the experience of those who have studied and created before us; the aim of this lesson is to receive the vitality of their inspiration and to continue their creative work in its original spirit, which thus, in a new generation, is born again with the freedom, the youthfulness and the promise that it originally possessed.

Many of the mental attitudes previously responsible for the vitality of the higher disciplines—such as art and theology—nowadays grown rigidly formal, have today found a home in the world of scientific research, whose very name reveals its wide scope. In this connection, Pascal's formula is very relevant and is manifestly the motto for the true scientist: "The entire succession of men, throughout so many centuries, should be thought of as one and the same man, ever-present and learning continually." [2] This well-known passage expresses, in its own way, an important aspect of the nature of tradition.

The "tradition" that is the subject of this little book is not scientific, artistic, sociological or even moral tradition; it is Christian tradition, in the dogmatic sense of the word. It was an advantage to introduce the reader to it on the basis of more familiar meanings. Yet the theological problem of

---

[2] Pascal, *Opuscules* (Ed. Brunschvig), p. 80.

tradition will not be entirely new to the reader, since the history of his country, and the conditions of life amid the religious divisions and entanglements of this world of ours will scarcely allow him to remain unaware of the existence of the controversy between Catholics and Protestants—the latter claiming the authority of Scripture alone, the former adding to it "tradition".

For every Catholic, Scripture (the Old and the New Testament) enjoys pride of place, since its value is absolute. Thus he knows that he is bound to read holy Scripture in a "Catholic Bible", even though he may be unable to say in exactly what way a Catholic Bible differs from a "Protestant" one. He knows that the Bible by itself, left to personal interpretation, may result in erroneous positions in Christian belief—the Christian sects remind him of this daily. He knows that since the Reformation there is controversy between Christians on "Scripture versus tradition", a controversy on the rule of faith. He knows that in the Catholic Church we do not refer exclusively to the Bible in a purely individual way; we read the Bible under the guidance of the Church and according to her interpretation; and so, while reliance on the Bible remains the supreme rule, it is not relied on as the Protestants rely on it, or as they are supposed to do. The Catholic lives on something else besides, even at those times and in those acts when he lives on the holy Scriptures. This something else is the Church, it is tradition; does this mean that the Church and tradition are equivalent, or even identical? In the first place tradition is something unwritten, the living transmission of a doctrine, not only by words, but also by attitudes and modes of action, that includes written documents, documents of the Magisterium, liturgy, patristic writings, catechisms, etc., a whole collection of things that form the evidence or monuments of tradition.

The most cultured of the faithful in religious matters are not unacquainted with this literature; they are aware or at least have some inkling of its existence. St. Augustine and St. Thomas Aquinas mean something to them, as do the Council of Nicaea and the Council of Trent. They know that Catholicism is not limited to the catechism and that its present form has its roots in a long past, rich in thinkers, saints and creative minds who have fashioned its culture, its devotion, its liturgy, and so on, and that the catechism itself is the fruit of a considerable development through the ages. By his possession of a faith that is personal, every Catholic with a minimum of culture is conscious of receiving an immense heritage at the hands of his Christian predecessors, although he has not made a detailed inventory, or even less a critical appraisal, of this inheritance. He is aware, in a way that is confused or precise to a greater or lesser extent according to the depth of his culture, that it contains much that is valuable and ancient, in varying degrees.

There are simple local customs, on occasion bordering on folklore, but there are also the decisions of the Councils and the succession of teachers whose commentaries enrich our religious culture. Instinctively, and also following the example of preachers who quote from them, we lend more authority to the most ancient writers, to those who lived, meditated and suffered during the years more immediately succeeding the apostolic age. The fact that they are near to the foundations seems to endow them not only with that solidity and venerable patina that endear ancient monuments to us, but with a kind of providential grace of authenticity, on the pattern of that bestowed on founders and pioneers. And so, reference to the primitive Church has enjoyed a privileged position at all periods of the Church's history. John XXIII referred to it on several occasions, notably in his first announcement of the Ecumenical Council and in his speech closing the Roman Synod.[3]

In the seventeenth century it was current to base the "perpetuity of the faith" on one or other of the articles of faith, the Real Presence, for example, or the primacy of the Pope. This was done by going through the testimony left by successive generations. Proofs of this kind, often reduced to two or three passages isolated from their historical and philological context, are to be found in our theological manuals, under the somewhat laconic heading *Probatur ex Traditione* (Proved from Tradition), following the heading *Probatur ex Scriptura* (Proved from Scripture). Today, however, this appeal to "tradition" is made in a new way; *ressourcement* (a return to the sources) is in fashion. This splendid word, coined by Charles Péguy, implies a return to the origins, or more often an advance to the present day, starting from the origins. This idea springs from Péguy's conception of revolution and reform as "the appeal made by a less perfect tradition to one more perfect; the appeal made by a shallower tradition to one more profound; the withdrawal of tradition to reach a new depth, to carry out research at a deeper level; a return to the source, in the literal sense".[4] Péguy also speaks of "the introspection that retraces its steps through human history".[5]

---

[3] Speech of January 25, 1959: "This fact arouses in the heart of the humble priest, who, in spite of his unworthiness, has been raised to his present position of Supreme Pontiff by the unmistakable will of divine Providence, a firm intention of returning to certain ancient forms of doctrinal pronouncements and wise rulings of ecclesiastical discipline" (*Documentation catholique*, 1959, col. 387). In his speech closing the Roman Synod, opposing certain possible excesses in regard to Marian devotion, John XXIII said: "We wish to invite you to keep what is the simplest and the most ancient in the practice of the Church" (ibid., 1960, col. 215).

[4] Preface to *Les Cahiers de la Quinzaine*, March 1, 1904.

[5] *Clio* 2: NRF [*La Novelle Revue Française*] (1932), p. 230.

Considered at this level, the problem of tradition, which we are to study, is not purely speculative and theoretical, and still less is it merely academic; even if it were it would still be worthy of our attention; it is fundamental to the present religious situation. For that situation is dominated on the one hand by the admirable effort toward renewal in the Church (though without essential change)—the stamp of the sound reforming instinct and of *ressourcement*—and on the other, by an ecumenical hope, enthusiasm and dialogue, which in the new climate of opinion has made the relationship between the Scriptures, the Church and tradition a topical problem.

The first object of this book will be to examine what every Catholic knows already about the tradition by which he lives, for the purpose of clarifying what is usually a confused view of the subject. Matters will probably appear more complicated than he had suspected. It will be impossible to avoid mention of the points at issue between our separated brethren and us, but I shall avoid all polemics, even with regard to those questions that were formerly the cause of the argument and the fuel which fed it. This dialogue, however, will necessarily be the confrontation of opposing views, but put forward in all fairness and mutual respect.

Footnote references have been kept to a minimum, but a more detailed treatment of the subject with full references will be found in my two-volume work *La Tradition et les traditions: Essai historique*, volume one, and *Essai théologique*, volume two (Paris: Fayard, 1960 and 1963). I refer to these on occasion, using the abbreviations EH and ET.

The principal abbreviations used in the footnotes are the following:

AH	*Adversus haereses* of St. Irenaeus.
Denz.	Denzinger-Bannwart-K. Rahner. *Enchiridion symbolorum et definitionum*. Freiburg: Herder, 1952.
EH	*Essai historique* (see above).
ET	*Essai théologique* (see above).
HE	*Historia Ecclesiastica* of Eusebius.
PG	*Patrologia graeca*. J. P. Migne, ed. 162 vols. Paris, 1857–1866. The first number is that of the volume, the second of the column.
PL	*Patrologia latina*. J. P. Migne, ed. 221 vols. Paris, 1844–1864. The first number is that of the volume, the second of the column.
ST	*Summa theologica* of St. Thomas Aquinas.

CHAPTER I

TRADITION AND TRADITIONS

At the outset it must be made clear that the word "tradition" has, in fact, different meanings, and only on reaching the end of the book will the reader realize all that the word implies; our task will consist mainly in distinguishing between the different aspects and various components of a rich and complex reality, and in identifying their reciprocal roles. This chapter, which starts our investigation, should provide us with the primary distinctions and essential definitions.

THE PRIMARY MEANING, BROAD YET PRECISE

"Tradition" comes from the Latin *traditio*, the noun of the verb *tradere*, "to transmit", "to deliver". It was a term of ratification in Roman law: for example, the legal transfer of a shop or house was accompanied by the act of handing over its keys, *traditio clavium*; the sale of a piece of land was accompanied by the act of handing over a clod of earth. *Tradere, traditio* meant "to hand over an object", with the intention, on the one hand, of parting with it, and, on the other, of acquiring it. *Tradere* implied giving over and surrendering something to someone, passing an object from the possession of the donor to the receiver. In Greek, *paradidonai*, aorist *paradounai*, had the same meaning. An equally good simile would be that of a relay race, where the runners, spaced at intervals, pass an object from one to the other, a baton, for example, or a torch.

Taken in its basic, exact and completely general sense, tradition or transmission is the very principle of the whole economy of salvation. Tradition, in this sense, encloses and dominates it completely, from its very beginning, which is none other than God; God as the word is understood in the New Testament, referring to the Father, the absolute Origin, the uncreated Principle, the primordial Source, not only of all things visible and invisible, but of the very divinity of the Son and the Spirit, by procession. God (the Father) then gives his Son to the world; he *delivers* him to the world. Here, the New Testament uses our verb "to deliver" to show that the Father did not spare his Son but gave him up for us (Rom 8:31–32), to show that the Son "gave himself up for" us (Gal 2:20; Eph 5:2, 25), and finally, to show that he delivered or bestowed his Spirit on John and on Mary, at the foot of the Cross, representing the Church (Jn 19:30).[1]

Thus the economy[2] begins by a *divine* transmission or tradition; it is continued in and by the men chosen and sent out by God for that purpose. The sending of Christ and of the Spirit is the foundation of the Church, bringing her into existence as an extension of themselves: "As the Father has sent me, even so I send you."[3] At the very time when the apostle John was transmitting these words of the Lord to the Church, Clement of Rome was writing: "The apostles have been dispatched to us by the Lord Jesus Christ like the bearers of good tidings. Jesus Christ was sent by God. Christ, therefore, comes from

[1] All the exegetes link Jn 19:30 with Jn 20:22 (the "Johannine Pentecost"); cf. 19:34.

[2] In ecclesiastical terminology "economy" is the name for the series of acts planned by God for the salvation of mankind. The Latin word is *dispensatio*.

[3] Jn 20:21; cf. 17:18; 1 Jn 1–3; Jn 10:14–15; 17:26; Lk 22:29, 31–33; cf. Rom 1: 1–6; 1 Cor 3:23; 11:3.

God, and the apostles come from Christ; these two acts result fittingly from God's will." [4] After Clement, Ignatius of Antioch, Serapion of Antioch and Tertullian made similar allusions to the fact that the divine economy reposes on a communication descending like a cascade from God through Christ and the apostles: "We must keep what the Churches have received from the apostles, the apostles from Christ and Christ from God." [5]

After these ancient witnesses, perhaps I may be forgiven for quoting a contemporary author who states this same Christian law of transmission in poetic language. Péguy wrote, in *Le Porche du mystère de la seconde vertu*:

Just as at the church door, on Sundays and feastdays,
When we go to Mass,
Or at funerals,
We pass holy water to each other from hand to hand,
One to another, one after the other,
Directly from hand to hand, or pass a piece of blessed
     bread dipped in holy water,
To make the sign of the cross, upon ourselves, the living,
     or on the coffins of the dead,
So that step by step the same sign of the cross is, as it
     were, carried by the same water. . . .
In the same way, from hand to hand, from fingers to fingers,
From finger-tip to finger-tip, the everlasting generations
Who go to Mass age after age,
One generation succeeding another,
Pass on the word of God, in the same hope,
In the same breasts, in the same hearts, until the world
     itself is buried.

---

[4] Clement, *Epist. 1 ad Cor.*, 42, 1–2.
[5] Tertullian, *Praesc.* 21:4, 37:1. Other references in EH, p. 96, n. 7.

Usually, when it is a question of handing over a material object, the donor loses possession of it and can no longer enjoy it. But this is no longer true when it is a question of spiritual riches—when a teacher transmits a doctrine, he commits it into the keeping of another, to be enjoyed by him, without losing any of it himself. This is very true of Christianity.

First, because it is above all a doctrine; what God transmits in his Son, what Christ delivers to his apostles, and the apostles to the churches, is in the first place the Gospel, the divine and saving doctrine that is the object of our faith. *Tradere*, in Latin, often means "to teach". Second, because Christianity is essentially a fellowship:

> That which was from the beginning, which we have heard, which we have seen with our eyes, which we have looked upon and touched with our hands, concerning the word of life—the life was made manifest, and we saw it, and testify to it, and proclaim to you the eternal life which was with the Father and was made manifest to us—that which we have seen and heard we proclaim also to you, so that you may have fellowship with us; and our fellowship is with the Father and with his Son Jesus Christ.
>
> —1 Jn 1:1–3

Tradition is an offering by which the Father's gift is communicated to a great number of people throughout the world, and down the successive generations, so that a multitude of people, physically separated from it by space and time, are incorporated in the same unique, identical reality, which is the Father's gift, and above all the saving truth, the divine Revelation made in Jesus Christ. Tradition is the sharing of a treasure, which itself remains unchanging; it represents a victory over time and its transience, over space and the separation caused by distance.

The reality that it communicates is primarily a doctrine, but not exclusively so. Indeed, if "tradition" is taken in its basic, strict sense, signifying transmission, or delivery, it includes the *whole* communication, excluding nothing. If, then, we consider the *content* of what is offered, tradition comprises equally the holy Scriptures and, besides these, not only doctrines but things: the sacraments, ecclesiastical institutions, the powers of the ministry, customs and liturgical rites—in fact, all the Christian realities themselves.

This inclusive meaning of the word has already been used in the past; Jacques Bossuet came very near to it when he wrote: "The tradition to which I allude here as interpreter of God's law, is an unwritten doctrine coming from God and preserved in the feelings and universal practice of the Church."[6] But this meaning was especially dear to the Catholic school of Tübingen toward the middle of the nineteenth century; it is favored by J. A. Möhler, 1825; F. A. Staudenmaier, 1845; and A. Tanner, 1862. At this period the Russian (Orthodox) *Long Catechism* also says: "By the word tradition is meant the doctrine of faith, the divine law, the sacraments and the liturgical rites, in so far as they are handed down by word of mouth and by example, from one man to another and from age to age."

Tradition in the strict sense

Among the Christian realities transmitted in this way, some are self-contained entities in themselves; this is true, in particular, of the holy Scriptures. The book exists objectively, in its own right, as does the actual text; both can be obtained and owned, without needing to be given by someone else. It

---

[6] *Défense de la tradition des saints Pères* (against Richard Simon and Ellies du Pin).

is true that the question still remains to know why the book is composed of *these* particular texts, and not others, and why it enjoys the absolute value given to the Word of God; I return to this question in chapter three. A written text exists independently of the living act of its transmission; the meaning of a doctrine, however, the solution it contains to a problem not yet encountered, the spirit of piety or Christianity itself, in its entirety, are possessed, in their pristine condition, only by reason of the living act of tradition.

Thus a certain distinction is made according to the elements or content of the deposit that is transmitted. But the immediate concern of this distinction is the inner reality, characteristic of tradition as we first defined it, that is, as a delivery or transmission. For, if an essential element of tradition is the handing over of an object from one to another, what exists in writing is not included as such, since it does not need to be passed from one to another in order to be possessed. That is why our first definition of tradition, which is authentic and formal, yet inclusive, must be followed by a second, equally formal, yet more precise and narrow, in which the distinction is made between tradition and what is written. This distinction is classic; it is not artificial, since it stems from a formal element of the notion of tradition. In this stricter sense tradition signifies transmission by some means other than writing.

At this stage, however, we cannot determine whether unwritten tradition contains different subject matter from that of written tradition, or whether it is the transmission of the same thing in a different way and under a different form. And so a new distinction or qualification appears possible within the formal and strict notion of tradition, according to whether "unwritten" and "by some means other than writing" simply refer to a mode or way of transmission other than writing, or to material objectively different from, or new to, what is otherwise contained in Scripture. For those who are slightly familiar with the history of this problem, this distinction will quickly show itself to be extremely important. We shall see in what follows that the Fathers of the Church, though aware of the transmission of things not contained in Scripture, favored the first explanation of tradition, as an original way of passing on the same objective material that is found in Scripture; since the Reformation, on the other hand, owing to the controversies resulting from it, tradition has often been claimed to include practices and doctrines for which Scripture provides no explicit authority. But, in fact, neither were the Fathers unaware of this second interpretation, nor has modern theology neglected the former. We can now try to identify them both more clearly.

Tradition as a means of communication other than by writing

In the last third of the fourth century, St. Basil, who put forward some profound ideas on the nature of tradition, said that it is *agraphos*, "unwritten"; simultaneously with the actual transmission of written doctrines, it adds something else to them, something of itself, a new modality other than Scripture. Understood thus as a means of communication, tradition is the transmission of the whole of Christianity, without distinguishing or favoring any one of its elements.

Christianity was not transmitted otherwise at first, except that it claimed to be the true fulfillment of the Scriptures: it was the fact or reality spoken of by Moses and the prophets. During roughly 150 years, what was called "the Scriptures" meant the Old Testament; as for the Gospel, it was preached "in conformity with the Scriptures" and was based on them. Yet after that time, there existed apostolic writings, Gospel accounts and epistles, all recognized as such. But in the earliest years of the Church, at a time when she was never more truly herself, there were neither letters by the apostles nor written accounts of what Christ had said and done. The Gospel was preached, and the Christian faith was handed on simply by "tradition".

In this connection one often hears of the Gospel that preceded the Gospels,[7] by which I mean the one that was imprinted in the hearts of the apostles by the living word of Jesus, and by the winning, penetrating and forceful unction of the Holy Spirit; this Gospel they understood when the Lord explained the Scriptures to them (Lk 24:44–45) and revealed its meaning to them, so that they themselves admitted understanding what they had witnessed only in the light of Easter, Pentecost and the corporate experience of the faith.[8] This is the Gospel that they preached, and by proclamation of which the first believers were converted and the first community of "saints" was formed, others springing up almost everywhere in its wake and taking it for a model. Within these communities, all relying on the witness of the apostles, experiences shared with the Lord were often recalled, and conclusions were reached and compared. It was there, and in that manner, that the Church realized all the implications raised by the man Jesus Christ, his coming on earth in the flesh, his death and Resurrection, his exaltation at the right hand of God, his presence among his own by his Spirit, his baptism and his Eucharist. In this way, the faith of the Church led the testimony of the apostles to a more explicit awareness of itself, and of all that it implied, even while this testimony was fashioning a corporate faith.

The inspired text of the Old Testament was already a reflection of the faith and meditation of the Jewish communities:

---

[7] See J. Huby, *L'Évangile et les Évangiles*, new ed. (Paris, 1954).
[8] Cf. Jn 2:19–22; 12:16; 13:7; 20:9; Lk 24:44–49.

our Pentateuch, in particular, seems like the final presentation of traditions gathered in such communities—for that matter, the text itself is the result of tradition. The same is true, in part, of the texts of the New Testament, to a greater or lesser extent, according to the nature of the writings, and the proportionate place given to the apostolic gift, or to the personality of the author. An entire school of exegesis, that of form criticism (*Formgeschichte*), set about discovering the role played by the milieu in the Judeo-Christian or Greek communities, and those in Jerusalem, Galilee and Antioch. A countercurrent in the flow of ideas has today corrected certain of the excesses and narrowness shown by this school, but the fundamental fact remains. It points to the priority of unwritten transmission over the written, and even to a certain dependence of the written text on oral transmission, and on the preservation of men's faith in their hearts.

In this method of transmission we must first situate the living word: the apostles were essentially witnesses, heralds of the Good News, preachers and teachers. The churches were established by the spoken word and organized in like manner; when St. Paul listed the ministries for building up the Church, he always speaks of the ministries of the word (see 1 Cor 12:28; Eph 4:11). The living example of the apostles, however, must also be given a place of importance. The Jewish ideal of discipleship entails far more than the mere learning that characterizes a pupil; it included the imitation of the master's life and habits. The disciple not only received oral lessons from his master, to be memorized—a most effective practice for inculcating "tradition", and one that Jesus certainly applied to his disciples—he also learned from his master's actions and personal way of life.

So it was with the apostles; they had not only heard Jesus teach, they had "followed" him everywhere; they had seen him praying, welcoming people and healing the sick; they had seen him celebrate the Last Supper and break bread after giving thanks to God. Immediately after Pentecost (cf. Acts 2:42, 46) and during the next thirty years, the Christians celebrated the Breaking of Bread, although no written text on the matter existed. The texts that were then written give very few details concerning the rite to follow or the method of procedure. It was enough for the apostles to have seen Jesus celebrate it. The Church, which had seen the apostles do it after him, thus learned the Eucharist from its actual celebration; and so it was for many other things. Jesus spoke only discreetly and briefly about chastity, but he left his example, in this matter, witnessed by his apostles, as they had witnessed the example of his Mother. Taught by this living experience, they assimilated it and taught it in their turn to the churches. They laid down rules in these churches, and especially in the one at Jerusalem, whose example was to some extent an expression of the apostolic model (see 1 Cor 14:33 ff.). They instituted ministers and laid down a communal discipline, and the Gospel passed through all this, being simply an authentic expression of the religious relationship or the Covenant in Jesus Christ by faith. The Gospel, this religious relationship, and Christianity in all this were propagated by means other than writing. By what means? By means of tradition.

Catholics believe that this method of communication is the one most essential to the Church, and that it would suffice if it alone existed. St. Irenaeus testifies to this, in approximately A.D. 180: "If the apostles themselves had left us no Scripture, would it not be necessary to follow 'the order of Tradition' that they have transmitted to those to whom they entrusted the churches? It is precisely to this order that many barbaric nations, who believe in Christ, have given their assent;

they possess that salvation written 'without ink' or paper 'by the Holy Spirit in their hearts' (2 Cor 3:3), and they keep the ancient tradition most carefully, believing." [9]

But St. Irenaeus knew that after *preaching* the Gospel, the apostles, "by God's will, have transmitted it to us in the Scriptures, so that it may become the foundation and pillar of our faith".[10] In fact, the economy, which expresses God's will, includes both tradition and Scripture; in the remainder of this book I shall try to specify the relationship and harmony existing between them, and their mutual complement and nature, which this economy implies.

Protestants are of the opinion that this twofold means of communication is invalidated by the existence of apostolic writings, recognized as her standard reference by the Church herself, by reason of the scriptural canon that she drew up. At least, if they admit the actual existence, and the possible advantages, of a certain tradition, they insist that, in laying down a scriptural canon, the Church has forfeited the use of unwritten tradition as a standard reference, with a value comparable to that of Scripture. (This is the position of O. Cullmann.) It is not evident, however, that the Church has given this meaning to the process by which she drew up, not without a certain hesitation, a list of canonical writings, which she considers as a norm (since they come from the apostles—or from their immediate collaborators, who were controlled and, as it were, endorsed by them). The list is, therefore, certainly linked to the apostles, but, as the texts show, those who compiled it were conscious of receiving the apostolic heritage from their "tradition", which was preserved in the Church by the succession of bishops. The

---

[9] AH, 3, 4, 1 and 2 (PG 7:856).
[10] Ibid., 1, 1 (PG 7:884).

Protestants show themselves such severe critics of the unwritten means of tradition only because they identify it with the transmission, by word of mouth alone, of teachings that seemed destined rapidly to lose their guarantee, since words are easily distorted, transformed and added to, whereas in the writings of the apostles we come into contact with their teaching exactly as it left them, down to the very words they used.

But when we speak of communication by some means other than writing, we think less of an oral transmission of an unwritten teaching than of transmission of the very substance of the Christian faith, which surpasses any written statement.

We can return now to the striking example of the Eucharist. The written teaching of the apostles about this mystery is contained in some thirty or forty verses. These are texts of an inexhaustible depth and richness, but, in addition to the fact that the Eucharist was celebrated and administered without waiting for them to be written, it is obvious that the faith of the Church goes far beyond what the texts contain. This faith was formed and continues to be formed in the successive generations of Christians, from the Eucharist itself, taken as a present reality, celebrated in the Church according to tradition. In order to share the faith of the apostles on this point, and to believe exactly what they believed, it is not so much a matter of reading, studying and interpreting their written teaching, as of partaking, in our turn, of the Bread and Wine in which the apostles communicated (for the first time from the hands of our Lord), followed by the whole succession of generations after them.

In the same way, to take another example, the Church's faith in the mystery of the Redemption is not reached by reading and studying the Gospel or apostolic texts in which the mystery is expressed, just as the apostles' faith was not the result of listening to the few words of formal instruction in which Jesus expounded it. They saw him in the guise of a suffering servant, without, at first, understanding the meaning of what they saw; they saw him on the Cross. The Church saw him—she contemplates him each day—on the Cross: gazing not from curiosity, avid only for information, but gazing with love, eager to understand, as only love can, and bringing her gaze continually back to the object of her love. By baptism, the Eucharist, even the humblest sign of the Cross, ceaselessly the Church celebrates the mystery of our Redemption. While light is shed, by her doctrine, on the reality of this mystery that she transmits, her teaching is illuminated reciprocally by the same reality, believed, loved, celebrated, lived and possessed.

We can look finally at the Church herself and her ministries. What has been handed down in writing on this subject is certainly considerable, and infinitely precious, but it is also fragmentary and sporadic. It is well known that the word "Church" itself occurs only twice in the Gospels (Mt 16:18 and 18:17), and that 1 Peter, while it deals at length with the idea, does not mention the word once. As for the ministries, they are mentioned more from an ethical point of view, with regard to the binding nature of their exercise within the community, than that of their organization. It is significant and worth noting that the same is true of the ordination rituals. But the scriptural evidence is of a nature to provide endless discussion, and in fact there has been so much argument over its exact meaning that a critical reader of the Bible can always produce reasons for doubting a given piece of evidence, for dating it differently, for attributing it to another writer who was stupid or biased, and so on. What are the "presbyters" and the "episcopos"; what is the origin of their institution?

The Church could not wait until the critics were agreed among themselves: she had to live. She lived her own life, which had been handed down to her as such, before the texts and together with them, in the texts and yet not limited to them, independently of them. She did not receive her life from them. She *was* the Church from the time of the apostles and not the product of their writings; she used these writings, not following them word for word, as a pupil copies an exercise imposed from outside, but treating them as a mirror and yardstick to recognize and restore her image, in each new generation.

Tradition, as understood in this paragraph, is the communication of the entire heritage of the apostles, effected in a different way from that of their writings. We must try to define it more precisely and describe the original way in which it was done. It was not by discursive means, with all the accurate and precise formulation that this allows; it was by means of the concrete experience of life and of the familiar everyday realities of existence. It could well be compared to all that is implied by the idea of upbringing as opposed to instruction. We do not bring up a child by giving him lectures in morality and deportment, but rather by placing him in an environment having a high tone of conduct and good manners, whose principles, rarely expressed as abstract theories, will be imparted to him by the thousand familiar gestures that clothe them, so to speak, in the same way that the spirit informs the body and is expressed by it. Education does not consist in receiving a lesson from afar, which may be learned by heart and recited, thanks to a good memory, but in the daily contact and inviting example of adult life, which is mature, confident and sure of its foundations; which asserts itself simply by being what it is, and presents itself as an ideal; which someone still unsure and unformed, in search of fulfillment and in need of security, will progressively come to resemble, almost unconsciously and without effort. A child receives the life of the community into which he enters, together with the cultural riches of the preceding generations (tradition!), which are inculcated by the actions and habits of everyday life. Max Scheler has defined this remarkably well in his analysis of the way in which what he calls the "models" behave differently from the "leaders". He writes:

> The second vehicle of active influence used by the models is called tradition. Tradition lies halfway between heredity and the mode of learning and education leading to "self-knowledge". It is communicated automatically with life itself. It consists in acquiring a certain mentality, certain habits in exercising the judgment and will, by coming into contact with, and unconsciously imitating, the behavior and way of life of the milieu. In short, with tradition—and it is this which characterizes it—we are not aware of receiving something. We take the will of another for our own; we make no judgment or evaluation before receiving it, and no choice is involved. We believe that we ourselves have noticed and chosen what is transmitted to us. But long before a child comes under the influence of intentional education and instruction, by his conscious imitation, his behavior, his mode of expression, his actions and all the things he has done automatically without knowing why, he has already in him the seeds and latent organism of his future personality.[11]

It is a higher form of instruction. St. Thomas Aquinas asks why Jesus did not spread his teaching by the written word. The first reason he gives is derived from the greatness, the transcendency even, of Christ himself. For "the greater the

[11] *Vorbilder und Führer*; French translation, *Le Saint, le Génie, le Héros*, trans. E. Marmy (Lyon-Paris, 1958), p. 36.

teacher, the more perfect should be his method of teaching. It was fitting, therefore, for Christ, who is the greatest of teachers, to engrave his doctrine in the hearts of his listeners, which is why we find in the Gospel of Saint Matthew (7:29) that he 'taught like one who had authority'. This also explains why the greatest among the pagan philosophers, Pythagoras and Socrates, preferred to write nothing. For is not, in fact, the object of writings themselves to engrave the doctrine in the hearts of the listeners?" [12] St. Thomas always goes straight to the heart of things. He says that Christ did not teach by means of the written word because he is the absolutely perfect Teacher. Indeed the highest form of teaching is that which most immediately and most perfectly fulfills the object of all teaching. But all teaching aims at reaching the "heart" of those to whom it is given, that is, at going beyond an intellectual understanding of an academic or scientific explanation to reach the conscience—that level of intimate appreciation and feeling, inseparable from our moral personality itself. It is in this sense that a milieu is educative. It forms a certain spirit in *us*, or rather it forms *us*, starting with our most elementary reactions, and guides us in a definite direction.

But a milieu exists only through, and by means of, people. For tradition to exist—tradition understood as the environment in which we receive the Christian faith and are formed by it—it must be borne by those who, having received it, live by it and pass it on to others, so that they may live by it in their turn. Tradition, like education, is a living communication whose content is inseparable from the act by which one living person hands it on to another. A written text, on the other hand, exists in its own right.

[12] ST, IIIa, q. 42, a. 4.

We may even discern a feminine and maternal touch in the vital aspect of tradition. A woman expresses instinctively and vitally what a man expresses logically. The man is the *logos*, the external agent. The woman is the recipient, the matrix and fashioner of life. She creates the surroundings in which life will retain its warmth; one thinks of the maternal breast, of tenderness, of the home. She is fidelity. The man is intended for the hazards of the struggle outside, where he may receive wounds and be at the mercy of adventure and inconstancy. In the woman he finds again the one who waits, keeping intact the warmth and intimacy of the home. Venturing beyond experience into the realm of literature, one thinks of Peer Gynt before his mother or Solweig; of *Christine Lavransdatter*, by Sigrid Undset; of *The Castle on the Hill*, by Elizabeth Goudge; of *The Citadel*, by A. J. Cronin.

A home or milieu possesses a wealth of strength and certainty found nowhere else. Both provide security and with it the possibility of expansion that security affords. Have we ever considered what we should be if we were completely isolated? We should be reduced to a poor sort of humanity, spending all our strength on assuring the essentials of life, and unable to plan any undertaking, however modest. The same would be true on an economic level, since we should be forced to earn our keep day by day; it would be true on a cultural level, since we should be limited to our personal experience; and it would be true on a religious level. How poor our faith would be, and how uncertain, if we were really left with nothing before us but the biblical text! And who would have given it to us, where would we have gotten it, how would we have found it? How poor and uncertain would be our communion with God, in Jesus Christ, if we were forced to establish it by ourselves, starting from ourselves and God alone, without the Church's maternal initiation, without the Christian community, without the communion of saints! What would become of our faith in the Holy Trinity without Athanasius and Nicaea? How should we pray without the Jewish psalms, without the liturgy, without the example and enthusiasm of the saints? We have received everything unconsciously, in the same way that we benefit from our culture, simply by being born and educated in a society whose culture was built up, treasured and handed down right to us.

One last characteristic of tradition as a living transmission is that, in this way, Christianity is possessed wholly and regarded as a totality, defying perfect comprehension and formulation; it also escapes external justification of a historical and critical nature. This particular point has been enlarged upon by Maurice Blondel in three articles. This is how they came to be written.

In rapid succession, books by Albert Houtin and Alfred Loisy had appeared. In 1903 the exegetical problem was placed before Catholic opinion as a choice between the traditional dogmatic pronouncements and textual criticism of the Scriptures, which employed, not only the same philological methods, but the same critical criteria and tests of authenticity as those currently used in any historical field.

Maurice Blondel, a lay philosopher whose charity made him particularly attuned to the Catholic spirit, entered the discussion by writing his series of three articles, the third of which remains [in 1964] one of the finest descriptions of tradition that exist. This third article, in particular, provided a decisive contribution, not only to the difficult problem raised, but to the notion of tradition.[13] For Blondel showed that, while it depends

---

[13] "Histoire et dogme: Les lacunes de l'exégèse moderne", in *La Quinzaine* 56 (January and February 1904): 145–67, 349–73, 433–58.

on the historical attestation, the Christian faith is not bound by it. Christianity has another source at its disposal, that of the ever-present *experience of reality*, to which the documents testify in their fashion. This experience itself is not shared by a few isolated individuals, but by a whole people, that is, the Church; and taken as a coherent whole it is an authentic means of reference. The transition from the material aspect of the historical evidence to the definitions of faith, a transition contested by the purely rational critics in the name of historicity, is actually effected by a living synthesis in which all the forces of the Christian spirit play their part: speculation, ethics, history—and this is tradition.

Blondel then went on to define this tradition: "It is not merely an oral substitute for the written teaching; it retains its *raison d'être* even in matters where Scripture has spoken; it is the progressive understanding of the riches possessed objectively from the beginning of Christianity, held and enjoyed in a truly Christian spirit, and transformed by reflection from 'something lived implicitly into something known explicitly'":

> Tradition brings to the surface of consciousness elements previously imprisoned in the depths of the faith and of its practice, rather than expressed, expounded and reasoned. So this conservative and protective force is also instructive and progressive. Looking lovingly toward the past, where its treasure is enshrined, tradition advances toward the future, where its victory and glory lie. Even in its discoveries it has the humble feeling of faithfully regaining what it possesses already. It has no need of innovation since it possesses its God and its all: but its constant task is to provide us with fresh teaching, because it transforms something lived implicitly into something known explicitly. Whoever lives and thinks in a Christian fashion is in fact working for tradition, whether it is the saint perpetuating the presence of Jesus among us, the scholar

returning to the pure sources of Revelation, or the philosopher engaged in opening the way to the future and ensuring the continual production of the Spirit of renewal. And this activity, shared by the different members, contributes to the health of the body, under the direction of its head, who, united to a conscience receiving divine assistance, alone orders and encourages its progress.

Blondel considered that a living fidelity would be more likely to keep the totality of the deposit intact right from the beginning than would a conscious and explicit record: "Action has the privilege of being clear and complete, even when it is implicit, while reflection, with its analytic character, only becomes a science after lengthy and hesitant consideration: and that is why it seems essential to me to relate dogmatic knowledge, which is never perfect, to the Christian life, which does not need an explicit science in order to reach perfection." There is nothing pragmatic about that; it is merely a recognition of the privileged position held by the Christian reality and the living fidelity enshrining it, and of its superiority over ideological assertions, fully analyzed and elaborated.

This value of totality has a further implication: it is not a question of a particular environment, but of a *catholic* [universal] one; it is not a question of adapting ourselves to a particular spirituality, to the values characteristic of one of the religious communities authorized by Catholicism—precisely because it is catholic. It is a question of adapting ourselves to whom our fathers held and what was held from generation to generation since the time of the apostles.[14] It is a question of becoming the beneficiaries of the apostles'

---

[14] St. Gregory of Nyssa, *Contra Eunomium*, c. 4: "The truth of our teaching is more than sufficiently attested by tradition, that is, the truth that has reached us from the apostles, having been handed down, like a heritage" (PG 45:653). Other texts in EH, p. 105, no. 4; ET, 1, sec. A, nos. 15–24.

heritage, or of the Gospel, as the Council of Trent calls it, handed down and communicated to us. St. Irenaeus, the glorious martyr-bishop of Lyons, wrote in approximately A.D. 180: "The Church, implanted throughout the universe and reaching the ends of the earth, has received from the apostles and their disciples this faith in one God, the Father Almighty." [15] "Having received this message and this faith, the Church, implanted as we said throughout the earth, keeps it most carefully, as though she formed a single household ... for though languages on the earth vary, yet the virtue (*dunamis*) of tradition is unique." [16]

The faith—we could even say Christian life—is something interior and personal; it is definitely not an individualistic principle of life, but a corporate and communal one, something we receive and in which we are incorporated and take part. We must believe and live like those who have believed and lived before us, since the apostles and Jesus Christ. The true religious relationship implies believing and living with our fellow men, for them and by them.

There is one action by which this communication is effected decisively and that reveals itself as the chief vehicle for tradition: this is baptism, where the faith is transmitted in its entirety—knowledge, principle of life and salvation, catechetics, sacrament and "mystery" in the sense of knowledge and in the sense of a saving act of God operating under sacred signs and apprehended by faith. The Fathers considered it an essential stage in the operation of "tradition"; St. Gregory of Nyssa calls it *prote paradosis*, the "first tradition" or "handing on". [17]

[15] AH, I, 10, I (PG 7:549).
[16] Ibid., 2 (PG 7:552).
[17] *Epist.* 24 (PG 46:1088D).

In the fourth century this aspect of transmitting the faith by baptism was expressed in a rite resulting from the liturgical organization of the catechumenate, whose origins go back to the fourth century. On a fixed day during the baptismal initiation, which lasted during the whole of Lent, the bishop *delivered* the text of the baptismal creed to the catechumen, explaining it phrase by phrase, and the catechumen had to "return" it to him eight days later, reciting it by heart. This was the double ceremony of the *traditio* and the *redditio symboli*, to which St. Ambrose and St. Augustine testify in the West, and the *Catecheses* of St. Cyril of Jerusalem (348) and *Pilgrimage of Etheria* bear witness in the East.

With a richness that defies analysis the patristic writings and ancient liturgies express a continuity—a profound unity even—between the faith conceived in the heart, nurtured progressively in the Church's maternal womb, professed at baptism, where we commit ourselves and are consecrated, by the ratification of the material rite of baptism, and the faith confessed before all and expressed as praise in the service of God. "It is necessary to be baptized according to what we have received by tradition (by transmission: *os parelabomen*), and to believe as we have been baptized, and thus to give praise as we believe." [18] As a believer took the necessary steps to enter into the community of the Church, going from height to height in the Christian life, the Lord's command constituting the apostolate and the Church was simultaneously fulfilled: "Go therefore and make disciples of all nations, baptizing them in the name of the Father and of the Son and of the Holy Spirit. . . . He who believes and is baptized will be saved" (Mt 28:19; Mk 16:16a). The apostolic faith, which is the very substance of tradition, was passed

[18] St. Basil, *Epist.* 125, 3 (PG 52:549B).

on; it was passed on as an objective reality, equally by verbal teaching, everyday discipline, instructive example, the entry into a community and acceptance of its rules and behavior, and finally by the material reception and efficacy of the sacrament. It is really and truly a communication of the whole Christian faith, and that is the profound meaning of tradition in the chief sense that we are here considering.

The process continued after baptism, throughout the Christian life—life in the Church—its elements maintained by the continuing action of the principles that gave the process birth. The Christian, born of the Spirit and of water administered with a verbal formula (Jn 3:5; Eph 5:26; Tit 3:5), was not subsequently left alone with the text of the Scriptures, which, it may be noted in passing, had also been "delivered" to him;[19] nor did his formation in the Church consist solely of catechetics and verbal instruction. The Church, the fellowship of the faithful of Jesus Christ, has the same structure as the material churches where the community gathers, a structure that might be described as "bipolar". She has a single center, Jesus Christ, who loves her as his own flesh (Eph 5:29) and feeds her with himself, the true Bread of Life, in two ways and under two forms: by the Bread of the Word, given from the pulpit, and by the Bread of the Sacrament, given from the altar.[20]

Although different, these two ways blend and converge and are meant by the Lord to be used in conjunction to obtain the *fullness* of life. When Ignatius, the martyr-bishop of Antioch,

[19] There existed a delivering of the Gospels, *traditio Evangeliorum*, for which the Gelasian Sacramentary (seventh century) gives a rite; the salient features of each of the four Gospels were briefly explained and the opening words of each were read. In Naples there existed a delivering of the psalms, *traditio Psalmorum*.

[20] See the author's study "Les deux formes du Pain de vie dans l'Évangile et la Tradition", in *Sacerdoce et laïcat* (Paris, 1962), pp. 123–59.

wrote the following in approximately A.D. 107, he was making no distinction between the sacrament and its spiritual fruit:
"faith which is the Lord's flesh and *agapē* which is the blood of
Jesus Christ".[21] All the early baptismal theology does the same.
There is no sacrament without words, and the celebration of
the liturgy itself is very instructive: it is the present announcement of the mysteries it commemorates, the fruits of which it
bestows. It is the most concentrated and efficacious element
of this propagation of Christianity that immediately concerns
us. The liturgical celebration is the chief influence in shaping
the Christian spirit, formed, as we have seen, by tradition. It
is unsurpassed for its arrangement of the biblical texts in a way
that reveals their consonance, which points in turn to the fullness of the salvation that they contain, by leading them to the
center of the complete Revelation. I shall develop these brief
remarks in chapter three, in defining the relationship that exists
between Scripture and tradition, and in chapter four, in studying the principal monuments of tradition.

The fruit or the result and what might be called the sum
total of tradition, in the objective sense that we have just
explained, is what the Fathers and the Councils have often
termed the "Catholic spirit" or the "mind of the Church".[22]
This idea can be interpreted in two ways, corresponding to
an objective or subjective sense.

In the objective sense it is the unanimous belief common
to the whole Church, considered not only from the aspect
of present-day Catholicity, but from that of its continuity,
and identity even, throughout the ages; it is the practice of
the faith common to the faithful today, to the preceding generations from whom they inherited it, and, through them,

[21] *Ad Trall*, 8, 1.
[22] See footnotes in ET, chap. 3, especially nn. 19 ff.

to the apostles and first Christians themselves. It is the heritage of the Catholic communion, a heritage that is truly "catholic" and total, which greatly surpasses the part that is recorded, and even more the part that we have understood and are capable of explaining. For, on the one hand, united with the totality, we hold all that it contains, and on the other, owing to its transmission, what we hold is not merely a theoretic statement, or even a profession of faith, but the *reality that is Christianity itself.* We received it with our baptism, the beginning of our initiation, and subsequently throughout our life in the Church, in the highest degree in the celebration of the Eucharist, by which Christ *delivers* himself to us; this reality is entrusted to our fidelity, with the injunction to keep and transmit it faithfully, without adding to it anything alien, taking anything away or changing its meaning.

In the subjective sense the *Catholic spirit* is a certain instinct, an intimate feeling or disposition, which springs from the awareness the Church has of her own identity and of what would threaten to change her identity, in the event of danger. No more need be said of this question here since it will be dealt with in the next chapter, which is devoted to the subject of tradition.

Tradition as a source of knowledge other than Scripture

This question has held an important place in the controversy aroused by the Protestant Reformation; it holds an equally important one in the criticism levelled at the Protestant principle of *sola Scriptura*, "Scripture alone".

Catholic apologists draw attention first to the fact that the Bible itself does not claim to be the exclusive rule of faith.

On the contrary, it supplies evidence of the existence of rules determining belief and conduct that are transmitted orally by the apostles. The Bible itself contradicts the rule it is supposed to represent. It is therefore impossible to uphold as exclusive a scriptural principle that is unknown and even contradicted by Scripture itself.[23] Neither Jesus, who wrote nothing, nor St. Paul ever said: "You will believe only what is written in the Gospels or in my letters", but we do find: "You will believe what has been transmitted and taught to you."

We should be prepared to find that the apostles had not recorded in writing all the rules that they gave the churches, in view of the fragmentary and occasional nature of their writings. What do the written documents we possess tell us of the preparation for baptism, of the eucharistic celebration, of the way to deal with sinners, and so on? St. John tells us that he has not written everything concerning Christ, at least with regard to his miracles (Jn 20:30; 21:25). The apostles preached before they wrote (cf. 1 Cor 15:1); they preached more than they wrote, and their letters speak of certain of their actions and speeches that are not recorded in writing.[24] St. Paul gave this advice to the Thessalonians: "So then, brethren, stand firm and hold to the traditions which you were taught by us, either by word of mouth or by letter" (2 Thess 2:15); he congratulated the Corinthians because they "maintain the traditions even as I have delivered them to you" (1 Cor 11:2); just as without repeating them he

---

[23] See A. M. Dubarle, "Écriture et Tradition: À propos de publications protestantes récentes", in *Istina* (1956), pp. 399–416. He remarks: "This using the opponent's own argument against him, expounded here, is outlined by St. Robert Bellarmine, Controvsiis, *De Verbo Dei*, lib. 4, c. 4, and by St. Francis de Sales, *Controverses*, pt. 2, chap. 2, Annecy ed., pp. 196–200."

[24] See 1 Cor 11:34; 1 Thess 5:1–2; 2 Thess 2:5, 15; 2 Jn 12.

reminded the Thessalonians of the instructions he had given them verbally (1 Thess 4:1–2; 2 Thess 2:15); finally he told the Corinthians that he would settle a certain number of points at his next visit (1 Cor 11:34).

The existence of unwritten apostolic traditions is therefore a certainty. It is equally certain that, recognized as such, they were observed by the Church and regarded as equally binding as the apostolic writings; since they had the same origin they enjoyed the same authority, except where their very nature showed them to be of minor importance. Protestants admit these two points, at least in theory, but they infer nothing from them. In fact they consider that such unwritten apostolic traditions have become too uncertain with the passage of time, too greatly adulterated with other elements, too difficult to locate and isolate, to be able still to act as rules that impose themselves on the Church. The Church, becoming aware of this at about the middle of the second century, is supposed to have laid down the principle of a scriptural canon, thus intentionally expressing the wish to submit all tradition "to the superior authority of apostolic tradition as codified in the holy Scriptures". This is especially the position of O. Cullmann.[25] I have criticized it

---

[25] He writes: "By the very fact of laying down the principle of a canon, the Church recognized that *from that moment* tradition was no longer a criterion of truth. She has drawn a line under the apostolic tradition. . . . This was certainly not in order to put an end to the continuing evolution of tradition. *But by an act of humility*, so to speak, she has submitted this subsequent tradition, of her own elaboration, to the superior authority of apostolic tradition, as codified in the holy Scriptures. Laying down a canon is equivalent to agreeing that from now on our ecclesiastical tradition needs to be controlled. And so it shall be—with the assistance of the Holy Spirit—by the apostolic tradition, fixed in writing; for we are in process of moving too far from the time of the apostles to be able to watch over the *purity of tradition*, without a superior written authority" (*La Tradition: Problème exégétique, historique et théologique* [Neûchatel and Paris, 1953], p. 44).

elsewhere, with regard to the meaning he attributes to the fixing of the canon.[26] This decision, which in fact became definitive only later on in the form of a completely exclusive list, was in no way understood by the Church to imply that she no longer recognized the authority of the unwritten apostolic traditions. On the contrary, the Church realized that she would hold the *fullness* of the apostolic heritage only by holding equally all of what she had received from the apostles that was not contained, at least explicitly, in the canonical Scriptures.

This is why all the churches of the third, fourth and fifth centuries, while claiming to hold the doctrine of the apostles, speak of their "traditions".[27] This does not always imply that a practice presented as containing an apostolic tradition is attributed to the apostles, *as such*. The example of St. Leo, studied by Fr. A. Lauras, simply shows that in many cases all that is meant is a mere indication traced back to the apostles and defined by subsequent pronouncements of the Church. The Fathers, however, enumerate a certain number of these unwritten apostolic traditions. Elsewhere I have drawn up a list, which is certainly incomplete, but significant and sufficient for our purpose, of what the Fathers, and then the medieval theologians, quoted as examples of such traditions, that is, particular points not actually found in Scripture (for, as we shall see in chapter three, firstly they admit a dogmatic tradition, consisting in the correct interpretation of the Scriptures). What, then, do we find—going back no further than St. Augustine, who died in 430?

---

[26] See EH, pp. 53 ff.

[27] Tertullian, *De Corona*, chaps. 3 and 4 (PL 2:98 ff.); St. Basil, *De Spiritu Sancto* 27 and 29, 71 (PG 32:193, 200); St. Epiphanius, *Panarion* 61, 6 (PG 41:1048).

—The Lenten fast: St. Irenaeus, St. Jerome, St. Leo;

—Certain baptismal rites: Tertullian, Origen, St. Basil, St. Jerome, St. Augustine;

—Certain eucharistic rites: Origen, St. Cyprian (water added to the wine in the chalice), St. Basil;

—Infant baptism: Origen, St. Augustine;

—Prayer facing the East: Origen, St. Basil;

—Validity of baptism by heretics: St. Stephen, St. Augustine;

—Certain rules for the election and consecration of bishops: St. Cyprian;

—The sign of the cross: St. Basil;

—Prayer for the dead: St. John Chrysostom;

—Various liturgical feasts and rites: St. Basil, St. Augustine.

From this we may conclude that it is, in fact, always a question of secondary points relating to some main reality itself clearly mentioned in Scripture; it is a question of interesting details concerning either liturgy and worship, or Church discipline and the Christian life; they are practical points of application and not articles of faith. Not, of course, that these points are uninteresting from a doctrinal point of view; it is obvious that infant baptism, the validity of baptism of heretics and prayers for the dead have dogmatic implications. They are less doctrines, however, than practical conclusions connected with doctrine, to determine Christian practice or the life of the Church according to the Gospel.

These precious comments of the Fathers prevent us from imagining oral apostolic tradition as the transmission of secret doctrines whispered from mouth to mouth from one generation to the next. In the first place, such an idea is a most unlikely fiction; what we know of history leaves no room for such a preposterous theory. In the second place, that idea contradicts the positive assurance of such ancient witnesses as St. Irenaeus and Tertullian that the apostles made public all that they knew, without keeping back a kind of esoteric or secret portion, as the Gnostics claimed to do.[28]

The testimony of the Fathers reassures us equally on further points. First, in certain matters, there existed several traditions, all apostolic—in the same way that there are four Gospels containing certain variations. The best-known example of this is the method of fixing the date of Easter; and yet this was a very important factor for the unanimity of the ecclesiastical body. According to St. Irenaeus, who treated the question,[29] these differences should not trouble the peace of the Church. There is all the more reason for ecclesiastical traditions to include variations consonant with this peace; the Catholic spirit, no less than that of the Gospel, favors a wise liberty with regard to certain of these traditions, which are mostly customs carrying the stamp, at times obsolete, of the period of their origin.

Second, a closer inspection of the testimony of the Fathers, St. Leo in particular, reveals that the "apostolic traditions" do not necessarily imply, in the eyes of the Fathers, that the rite or practice in question was instituted materially or historically by the apostles in its *present* form; it was sufficient that the apostles had given general directives, for which the churches, or the pastors of the Church, had formulated precise instructions. It was possible that the element attributed to the apostles had become hard to identify with the passage of time. St. Augustine, St. Jerome and St. Prosper held that a tradition was guaranteed as apostolic if it was universally known and accepted, and, further, if it was not formulated

---

[28] See references in EH, p. 112, n. 63.

[29] See St. Irenaeus' letter to Pope Victor in Eusebius, HE, 5, 24, 9–17; St. Irenaeus distinguished the importance of the questions (AH, 3, 4, 1).

in Scripture or defined by a full council.[30] A thousand years later Bellarmine put forward some rules for identifying such traditions; they were more complicated but still very broad. Since today we have more ample documentation at our disposal, and a more exacting biblical approach, we should be more critical of certain examples given by St. Augustine and others. Nevertheless, contemporary studies, especially those dealing with the development of the liturgy, give increasing weight and credibility to the theory that ascribes an apostolic origin to the liturgical and disciplinary practices of the early Church.[31]

It is rare, in fact, for the most important of these "traditions", whose origin is very probably apostolic, to have no connection with Scripture. Very solid connections are even revealed by searching the Scriptures, not so much for passages supporting each particular point immediately and critically, as for indications of the overall sense of God's actions and will. This is the method adopted by the liturgy, the Fathers and the Bible itself in its treatment of the earlier passages in the light of the later ones.[32] Take the Lenten fast, for example, or the habit of kneeling to pray or of facing toward the East, or even infant baptism and prayers for the dead; all these practices are not found *as such* in Scripture, but it would be easy to find analogies to support them, and hints and presages in the Bible. What follows, in fact, will show us that apart from certain most exceptional ecclesiastical traditions—and not always even then![33]—there is not a single point of belief that the Church holds by tradition alone, without any

[30] Texts in EH, p. 108, n. 24.

[31] A few indications will be found in EH, p. 111, n. 60.

[32] This has been shown in EH, pp. 76–91.

[33] G. Le Bras has shown that the canonical definitions of the *Decretum* by Gratian follow the scriptural indications literally, at times even as to their order.

reference to Scripture; just as there is not a single dogma that is derived from Scripture alone, without being explained by tradition.

This contention, whose truth is recognized by the best of the recent studies treating these questions, is likely to temper the violence of a recent discussion on the exact implication of the decree of the Council of Trent concerning tradition or traditions. Here is the text of the decree:

> The Holy Council . . . having ever before its eyes the removal of error and the preservation of the Gospel in its purity in the Church—the Gospel which, promised beforehand by the prophets in holy Scripture, our Lord Jesus Christ first promulgated by his own mouth and then ordered to be preached by his apostles "to every creature" as being the source of all salutary truth and moral life; realizing, too, that this same truth and code of morals is contained in written books and in unwritten traditions which, received by the apostles from Christ's own mouth or at the dictation of the Holy Spirit, have come to us, delivered to us as it were by hand; this same Council, following the example of the orthodox Fathers, reverently receives with like devotion and veneration all the Books of the Old and New Testament alike . . . as well as traditions concerning both faith and morals, as given us by Christ by word of mouth or dictated by the Holy Spirit and preserved in the Catholic Church by unbroken succession.[34]

Properly to appreciate the content and full meaning of this important text, a fine one despite its clumsiness and length, it is of capital importance to analyze briefly its sequence of ideas and structure. According to this passage the content of tradition is the *Gospel* promised by the prophets, made known by Jesus Christ and preached by the apostles as the (unique)

[34] Sess. 4, c. 1, April 8, 1546: Denz., 783.

source of all truth and all that is necessary for salvation. The Gospel is contained *both* in the Scriptures *and* in the *divine* or *apostolic* traditions relating to faith and morals, which have reached us, handed down as it were from hand to hand.

The first draft submitted to the Fathers of the Council stated that the Gospel in question was found and handed down to us partly in the holy Scriptures and partly in unwritten traditions: *partim . . . partim*. This draft stated that, from an objective or material point of view, the saving Gospel was only partially contained in the Scriptures, which needed completing, even at their very source, by oral apostolic traditions, and that certain truths necessary for salvation were not contained in the Scriptures.

Even though the expression *partim . . . partim* was finally replaced by a simple *et*, the Council of Trent was fairly generally interpreted in this sense by the authors largely responsible for debating the difficulties of this question in the generation that followed the Council; they include such theologians as Melchior Cano (*De locis theologicis*, posthumously, 1563),[35] St. Peter Canisius (*Catechism*, 1555),[36] and St. Robert Bellarmine (*Controversies*, 1586).[37] This interpretation is still accepted today by numerous theologians. But an equally large number of outstandingly talented theologians[38] have been, or are, of the opinion that it remains permissible after

[35] A recent study by H. Horst, in *Trierer Theol. Zeitschr.* (1960), pp. 207–23, shows, however, that Cano admitted the (material) sufficiency of Scripture to provide the truths necessary for salvation.

[36] See J. R. Geiselmann, in *Die mündliche Überlieferung* (Munich, 1957), pp. 170 ff.

[37] Ibid., p. 173.

[38] Dobmayr, 1841; J. E. von Kuhn, 1858 and 1859; J. H. Newman, 1845 and 1865; M. J. Scheeben and even J. B. Franzelin. In our own day [1964], G. Proulx; M. Schmaus; P. A. Liégé; A. M. Dubarle; J. Ratzinger; O. Semmelroth; H. Holstein; H. de Lubac, S.J.; E. Stakemeier; K. Rahner; and G. Tavard.

the Council of Trent, as it was before, to maintain that the saving Gospel is contained entirely in the Scriptures, as it is also contained entirely in tradition. This is the position I shall adopt, subject to certain qualifications, which I shall add in the remainder of this chapter and in the following ones. This position was considerably strengthened from a historical point of view, recently, by studies pursued by Professor J. R. Geiselmann of Tübingen.[39]

He has shown that there were two currents of thought dividing the theologians at Trent on the point in question, at a deeper level than their substantial agreement. This agreement concerned the respect for the traditions in the Church, which were reaffirmed to counter the Protestant denial of this position. But some theologians accounted for the addition of traditions by an objective or material imperfection in the Scriptures; it was this that they understood by *partim . . . partim*. The others remained faithful to the old conviction that had divided the Fathers and the entire medieval school, according to which Scripture contained, in one way or another, all the truths necessary for salvation. The Council, anxious to avoid taking sides in this question that divided Catholic opinion, finally solved the matter by replacing the expression *partim . . . partim* by an inoffensive *et*, which merely stated that "it is necessary to consult *both* the Scriptures and tradition" (Holstein), without imposing the idea of two sources, each of which would have been incomplete and, in this sense, insufficient.

No doubt those who accepted this vague expression *et* neither saw nor implied all that we understand by it; it seems that the majority continued to understand it in the *partim . . . partim* sense; we must therefore, on a historical count, side

---

[39] In *Die mündliche Überlieferung* (1957), pp. 123–206.

with those who criticized Professor Geiselmann, chiefly Fr. H. Lennerz. But this is not enough to invalidate this interpretation from a theological point of view, which is what interests us most here. For it remains true that the text of the Council does not have the *partim . . . partim*, but *et*, and that *as it is presented to us* it authorizes the interpretation of the professor from Tübingen, which has been corroborated by powerful intellects, including qualified historians.

Although important, the historical analysis of the question with its array of quotations must not be allowed to dominate and conceal its real significance, which history also helps to discover. And its real significance, to which the continuity of tradition bears witness, is that no article of the Church's belief is held on the authority of Scripture independently of tradition, and none on the authority of tradition independently of Scripture. Even the Marian dogmas defined in recent times, namely the Immaculate Conception and the corporal Assumption of the Mother of God, are stated, in the bull *Ineffabilis* and the constitution *Munificentissimus Deus*, which proclaimed them respectively, as not being without foundation in holy Scripture. Chapter three of this book, which examines this question on its own account, will amplify its basic principles. I mention it here simply in connection with the existence of unwritten apostolic traditions, as defined by the Council of Trent. The Council's aim was to defend this statement against the Protestant Reformers[40] and to assert the value of these traditions. Since the traditions in question are apostolic they are as respectable as the apostolic Scriptures (*pari pietatis affectu*). To deny their validity would be to

---

[40] The Reformers' position contained reservations but also admitted such naïve statements as the following by Luther: "All that is not found in Scripture is an addition by the devil" (*Treatise against the Mass*, [1521]).

disregard and neglect one of the two great ways in which the
Church of today and of all times is linked to the apostles,
who were chosen, predestined, sanctified and equipped to
be her founders by the spreading of the Gospel.

The Council of Trent spoke only of *apostolic* traditions. It
appears, however, that several Council Fathers and theologians made no very clear distinction between these and *ecclesiastical* traditions or customs, brought into being by the
Church during her history without having been received from
her founders at her origin.[41]

I spoke first of all of tradition as the transmission of the
reality that is Christianity: this is really *the* tradition. It is apostolic by origin, then ecclesiastical by its actual transmission.
I then spoke of apostolic traditions: these are also apostolic
by origin. There exist, likewise, numerous traditions that are
ecclesiastical by origin, having been laid down by the Church
during her historical existence: institutions, rites, customs,
discipline. Sometimes these are the historical form, or modification, perhaps, of a reality that is apostolic or even divine
in origin. For example, the obligation of hearing Mass on
Sunday or of the annual Easter Communion is an ecclesiastical modification of a divine or apostolic reality. The papacy,
in the form fixed by centuries of history, is a historical form
of a divine institution (that of Peter as supreme pastor and
head of the apostolic college), itself already modified by an
apostolic initiative (the fact that Peter had his "see" at Rome).
Sometimes ecclesiastical traditions are purely ecclesiastical.
Lastly, they can be a historical development of something
already begun by the apostles, but which is now impossible

---

[41] This point shows that the final and formal definitions of a Council may
be relatively independent of the personal opinions of the Fathers, though this
deprives them of none of their interest in the discussion between Professor
Geiselmann and his opponents.

to reconstitute in its apostolic state; such, for the most part, is the case of the sacramental rites.[42]

It will be noticed that there is often an involvement of the ecclesiastical traditions with the divine or apostolic, to such an extent that the distinction between them is as difficult to establish in practice as it is clear (and important) in theory. This state of affairs favors and even compels respect when taken as a whole. The critical mind may be unsatisfied, but after valid and necessary distinctions have been made, it should realize that, all things considered, this relative confusion is in fact explained by the nature of things.

In order to help the reader to find his way through the standard scholarly works dealing with tradition, should the need arise, I conclude this chapter by adding a few indications of the principal distinctions current in this subject:

1. *Active* tradition: act by which the agent of tradition, the Magisterium, in particular, transmits the deposit of faith. *Passive* tradition: the content, what is transmitted.

2. According to the origin or the author (who is the agent of active tradition) a distinction is made between *divine, apostolic* or *ecclesiastical* traditions.

3. According to the subject matter or content (therefore to do with passive tradition), a distinction is made between what concerns *faith* and what concerns *morals*, the latter being understood in the broad sense of "behavior", thus including ceremonies, ways of conducting them, and practical or disciplinary rules.

4. With regard to their duration, traditions can be perpetual or temporary and, of their nature, obsolete. Of course, this applies only to traditions in general. But Church

---

[42] Similar remarks were made at the Council of Trent.

tradition (often written with a capital) is subject neither to diminution or devaluation.

5. With regard to their scope and validity, traditions can be *universal* or *particular* and *local*. This is evident when it is a question of discipline or liturgy. But there are doctrinal traditions, belonging to different schools, which, without being physically linked to a place, have in themselves a restrictive value.

CHAPTER II

THE SUBJECT OF TRADITION

"Subject" corresponds to object or content. At the end of the last chapter, we saw the classical distinction between active tradition and passive tradition, that is, between the act of transmitting and the thing or object transmitted. The two are correlative. The act of transmitting implies a content, an object; it also implies someone who transmits, an active subject. The subject of tradition is the living being who carries it and is answerable for it: the subject of an action always bears a measure of responsibility.

In this chapter, I shall try to answer the following questions: Who carries tradition? Who is responsible for it? In what way and under what conditions? Once again we shall have to distinguish in order to avoid confusion. As we know already, tradition may be considered at different stages: at its point of origin, when the deposit of faith was established, and at the stage when the established deposit is communicated through time and space. There are differences between these two stages, and yet there is a continuity.

The differences are of a qualitative nature. For if the first stage is one of *delivery*, only the second is one of actual transmission. The first stage concerns Revelation seen as something unique, accomplished once and for all; the second stage is not lacking in Revelation, in the sense that a "spirit of Revelation", as the New Testament calls it, the Holy Spirit, is ever active in this stage to actualize the Word of God in the Church, but it is also filled with the active presence of what God has accomplished once and for all at the time of the prophets, of Christ and of the apostles. These last were the subject of the tradition that constitutes the deposit; the Church is the subject of the transmission of this deposit, which, as we shall see, is indeed something quite different from the passive object of a purely mechanical transmission.

Other differences exist within each of these two main stages. The prophets, by which is understood here the inspired men of the Old Testament, have not received the same fullness of grace as the apostles. We apply the role of prophet to Christ, but he possessed and filled it in the fullest and most perfect manner, since the authority of his teaching, however human in form, is the authority of *God* himself. On the Mountain of the Transfiguration Moses and Elijah (representing the law and the prophets respectively) vanish: raising their eyes, the apostles see no one but Jesus, and they hear the Father's voice: "This is my beloved Son, with whom I am well pleased; *listen* to *him*." Since he is the Word of God in its entirety, it is with reference to Jesus Christ that the prophets and apostles are considered as instruments of Revelation. Jesus Christ is he "toward whom the two Testaments are turned, the Old in expectancy, the New taking him as its model, both regarding him as their centre".[1] From another point of view, within the Church certain differences make themselves felt between the hierarchy and the body of the faithful; we shall point them out later.

[1] Pascal, *Pensées*, fragments, 740.

In spite of these differences, however, a real and definite continuity exists between the two stages we have indicated, and within each of them. It is the continuity of the divine economy itself, but it is not simply the continuity of a transcendent plan existing in the mind of God. Like the economy itself, it has a concrete reality (which could be called "physical" in the scholastic sense of the word) composed of a body and soul. The body is the mission and the soul the Holy Spirit. Jesus himself presented the mission of the prophets as part of the same divine mission to the world upon which he was sent.[2] As for the mission of the apostles, he gave it to them himself, as a continuation of the one on which he was sent by the Father: "As the Father has sent me, even so I send you" (Jn 20:21; cf. 17:18). After the apostles, the Church is naturally the next to benefit from the revealing and redemptive work of Christ, but she is also destined to be its instrument, the means by which it is communicated to the world. The New Testament sees her as living by the Incarnation, but also as having received its driving force and as being its prolongation until Christ returns in his power and glory.[3] The singleness of this mission is responsible for uniting those who have received it into a single moral body of emissaries and witnesses, each in his own place, according to the diversity of situation. In this regard we may speak of a unique subject of tradition, including its source even, and coming right down to us, like a wave unfurling from its point of origin to the shore. The source is the prophets and the apostles as witnesses of Jesus Christ; it is also Jesus Christ as

---

[2] See the parable of the murderous vinedressers in Mt 21:33 ff. and the parallels, and the warnings to the apostles in Mt 10:17–25; Lk 6:22–23.

[3] See R. Brêchet, "Du Christ à l'Église: Le dynamisme de l'Incarnation dans l'Évangile selon saint Jean", *Divus Thomas*, 56 (1953): 67–98; and also the author's book, *Pentecôte* (Paris: Cerf, 1956).

witness of the Father—"He who has seen me has seen the Father" (Jn 14:9); "My teaching is not mine, but his who sent me" (7:16)—it is finally God himself, the Father, the uncreated Principle, from whom the mission of Christ proceeds, as does the very being of the Word, who became man in Jesus Christ. It was a principle accepted by the Jews that the authority of the sender was communicated to the person he sent. The New Testament gives us many instances of this: "He who hears you hears me"; "whoever receives me receives him who sent me" (Lk 10:16; 9:48; Mt 10:40; Mk 9:37; Jn 13:20).

The view of tradition held by the Fathers of the Church is a very concrete and realistic transposition of certain passages in the New Testament where the mention of mission occurs. Tradition is a transmission of the faith and Christian life, which in our own lives is transformed into Christian behavior, profession of faith before men and praise of God.[4] The Catholic Church simply and really believes that once, and once only, God established a missionary body in the world, a reality set up publicly by divine right. Publicity is one of the characteristics of Revelation, whether it is considered in its prophets, in the Gospel, or in the apostolate and the Church, born at Pentecost. Founded by God, this body really exists in the world, the carrier and

[4] In this connection the following two major texts come to mind: "All authority in heaven and on earth has been given to me. Go therefore and make disciples of all nations, baptizing them in the name of the Father and of the Son and of the Holy Spirit, teaching them to observe all that I have commanded you; and lo, I am with you always, to the close of the age" (Mt 28:18–20); and: "For man believes with his heart and so is justified, and he confesses with his lips and so is saved. . . . But how are men to call upon him in whom they have not believed? And how are they to believe in him of whom they have never heard? And how are they to hear without a preacher?" (Rom 10:10, 14).

transmitter of what he has delivered to the world for its life and salvation.

THE HOLY SPIRIT: TRANSCENDENT SUBJECT OF TRADITION

The stability of this body results from the stability it receives from its divine institution; and it has received from God a soul consonant with its structure: the Spirit of God. This Spirit, the bond of love between the Father and the Son, is also the strong link between God and his external activity in establishing a fellowship between himself and mankind. "He has spoken through the prophets", we sing in the Creed. He was the driving force of the public mission of Jesus Christ himself, which consisted of Revelation (cf. Lk 3:21–22; 4:14) and salvation (cf. Heb 9:14; Rom 1:4). It is he who animates the apostles and the Church from within, to enable them to carry out the work with which they are entrusted. Among the works of the Spirit the New Testament insists especially on unification and bearing witness, which appear fundamental.

"Bearing witness" is a biblical and New Testament theme of a profound richness.[5] As always the Hebrew word that expresses the idea, and whose connotations underlie the passages in the New Testament, is remarkably instructive. Its root signifies "to repeat", as one repeats hammer strokes to drive in a nail or as one repeats a lesson to drive it into the mind and memory. This is why the word is fitting to express the idea of wishes or commandments, as we see

[5] The best works on this are R. Asting, *Die Verkündigung des Wortes im Urchristentum* (Stuttgart, 1939); A. Rétif, *Foi au Christ et mission* (Paris: Cerf, 1952), pp. 33 ff.

time and again in Old Testament passages where God's wishes
and commandments are called his testimonies (the Ark of
the Testimony is the ark from which God governed his
people by revealing his wishes to Moses). "To bear witness" in the Bible also assumes a dynamic sense of affirmation that imposes itself in the face of all opposition. A witness
is someone who announces God's will and plan of salvation
in spite of opposition, whose supreme reference is Jesus
Christ "put to death for our trespasses and raised for our
justification" (Rom 4:25). To bear witness is to announce
Jesus Christ, not only as a historical event that happened in
the past, but as the meaning of the present, each day, today
and tomorrow until the end of time. In the witness of the
New Testament there is much more than an account of the
past; there is the affirmation of an offered Covenant, sealed
in Jesus Christ, from this day forward, in the ever-present
circumstances of history, moving ceaselessly on. Witness,
apostolate and mission are closely linked. The Holy Spirit
is the active principle transforming them from within into
the means of realizing the history of salvation. Seen in the
perspective we have just sketched briefly in outline, the
New Testament texts assume a clear and definite meaning.
Let us recall the main ones.

The Spirit is promised and given to the apostles and, in
them, to the Church, so that they may be witnesses to the
ends of the earth and the end of time (Acts 1:8). To realize
this, in fact, the apostles are filled with the strength of the
Spirit, as are Stephen, Philip, their collaborators, their successors and all those who must carry the constantly renewed
spirit of testimony. He produces in them, and in all believers, the inner assurance of God's active presence: he testifies
within them, supporting and strengthening them in their stand
against the opposition of the world and the uncertainty of

their own hearts.[6] He reminds them of the meaning of the Gospel in detail, "all that I have said to you" (Jn 14:26); he guides them into all truth and ceaselessly leads this truth toward what is still to come (Jn 16:12–13). In doing this, he bears witness to Christ (15:26), he bears witness conjointly with the apostles, concelebrating as it were in the witness they bear (cf. Jn 15:26–27; Acts 5:32), to such an extent that, when the apostles make a definite decision concerning the life of the Church, they use this expression, which reveals all the calm assurance brought by the Paraclete: "For it has seemed good to the Holy Spirit and to us" (Acts 15:28).

In all this the Holy Spirit is not acting personally in the sense that his work is new or different from Christ's; he realizes and gives an inner depth to *what* was said and done once and for all by Christ, which is the Gospel (cf. Jn 14:26; 16: 12–13). The grace and truth of the Gospel has been fixed once and for all, at least with regard to its essential features, in the historical and visible mission of the incarnate Word, that is, by Jesus Christ; the Gospel determines the structure of the new and eternal Covenant; it is useless to expect or create other forms. This unique and particular event, which is nevertheless accessible to all times and which must be spread throughout the world and through history, being applied to an infinite variety of people and situations, is an essential feature of the economy of salvation. The special task of the Spirit is to ensure from within that many different people down the centuries and scattered over the surface of the globe share in this unique form of truth and life. He is able to do this, being "Spirit", that is, a presence that is ethereal and not bound by frontiers, at the same time universal and interior. But since he is the Spirit *of Christ*, his work is Christ's;

[6] See Rom 8:15–16, 26; Jn 16:6–15.

he simply realizes and infuses his personality into the Gospel
form of saving truth and life laid down and instituted on
earth by Christ, who watches over its accomplishment, seated
henceforward "at the right hand of the Father". By the Spirit
this institution becomes thus a perpetual "event", present
and active. There is a meeting and union between a present
action by God that is immediate and vertical, so to speak,
and the transmission of the framework of the Covenant by a
historical and visible succession, which is horizontal, as it
were: in exactly the same way that in a personal act of faith,
the external communication of defined truths effected by a
visible succession of ministers (who after Christ form a single missionary body) meets and fuses with an inspiration or
spiritual force that is received immediately and "vertically"
from God in the innermost depths of our hearts.[7]

In this way the identity of the Gospel, laid down once
and for all but intended to fill the world, all people and the
whole of history, in their infinite variety, is assured, externally, by the permanence of the form—the form of doctrine, sacraments, mission and ministries—and, internally,
by the personal identity of the Holy Spirit. For the Church,
for preaching or bearing witness to the Gospel, he is the
profound and transcendent principle of *identity*, since,
unchanging and unique, he is the Church's operative principle. His function as unifying principle is bound up with
this same role. Unity is the identity achieved in the lives of
men who do not fuse together to form a physical or concrete unity, since each is a person radically spiritual and
free, but who are united in a spiritual fellowship. It is the
Holy Spirit who promotes this fellowship from within, just

---

[7] This is also true of Scripture taken as the Word of God addressed to us
here and now; see the author's *Essai théologique*.

as its form preserves it externally; it is a fellowship of all the members one with another in the same truth, the same Lord, and the same action. Christians are baptized in the same Spirit to form a single body (1 Cor 12:13; Eph 4:3–6); each has received from the same Spirit the gifts that work for the common good (1 Cor 12:7) and aim at building up the frame of Christ's body (Eph 4:12; cf. 1 Cor 12:12–30). Many more references could be added if the subject were being treated for its own sake.

The New Testament texts are so positive that we cannot do better than to summarize them in the traditional expression describing the Holy Spirit as "the soul of the Church". But this expression must be understood correctly. The Holy Spirit does not form a substantial and physical or concrete union between us and God any more than he does between us and our fellow believers; he creates a fellowship of persons. It is true that according to God's promise he is bound to the form instituted by God himself (of which Scripture is one). He will never fail the Church, the mission or the authentic use of the sacraments found in the Gospel; he guarantees them an indefectible truth. It is impossible, however, to talk of their absolute impeccability, as we can, and should, for Christ. For Christ really *is* God, as well as really being man. In him the union of the divine and the human natures is a substantial one, within his very being. This is true neither of any one of us nor of the Church, although, in her own right, she has received promises given to none of us. There is no "incarnation" of the Holy Spirit in the Church like the Incarnation of the Word of God in Jesus Christ; there is simply a Covenant between them, guaranteed by God's absolute fidelity, as between two persons who do not form a single physical, existing reality, but retain their liberty. With the exception of a final indefectibility that God

has promised it, the ecclesiastical body, whose soul is the
Holy Spirit, remains fully human and historical. And so, to
speak of the Holy Spirit as the Church's soul and the transcendent principle of her identity, does not mean that *all*
that happens in the historical life of this Church is guaranteed by the Holy Spirit. There is a kind of subtle and complex gradation in what might be called his commitment in
the human aspect of the history of salvation, ranging from
his perfect gift to Christ to the laborious gropings of the
theologians and passing by the graces given to the apostles,
prophets, Fathers and great pontiffs or religious founders.
History offers many expressions and developments that are
doubtful, or simply less successful, in the realms of theology,
devotion and government. This does not dispense the teaching Church from constant reference to the fundamental teaching; on the contrary, it compels her to it, since the assistance
and positive inspiration that she receives, far from freeing
her from the necessity of human activity, operates within
this very activity.

If there were to be a continuation in the assistance of the
Spirit promised to the apostles in the historical and public
body of the Church, it is scarcely possible to see how this
could have been expressed better and in any other way than
by the innumerable texts that speak incessantly of it throughout the centuries, from the patristic and medieval ages down
to our own time. It is to the Holy Spirit, to his "revelation"
and "inspiration", that they attribute all the activity by which
spiritual men and the doctors or pastors of the faithful have
understood God's Word and have defended and explained it in
the face of heresy; also the decisions of the Councils by which
the faith of the Scriptures, the apostles and Fathers has been
defined, and the discipline of the holy life of God's People
has been laid down precisely; and the choices and decisions

by which the Church acquires leaders and guides herself through the vicissitudes of time.[8] Tradition, which is the transmission of the Gospel in and through the Church from Christ and the apostles, might be called the identity of the Gospel or of the Covenant sealed in Jesus Christ, in the Church; this tradition is equally attributed to the Holy Spirit, as to its most profound and definite, though "transhistorical", subject. Here is a frequently quoted passage by St. Irenaeus:

> The Church's preaching is everywhere the same and remains equal to itself, relying, as we have shown, on the testimony of the prophets, apostles and all the disciples, throughout the whole divine economy from beginning to end, throughout the usual activity [of God] which realizes Man's salvation and is an integral part of our faith—a faith which we receive from the Church and keep; a faith which, under the action of the Spirit of God, ever rejuvenates the vessel that contains it, like a costly liqueur preserved in a high-quality flask. . . . For where the Church is, there also is the Spirit of God; and where the Spirit of God is, there is the Church and all her grace. And the Spirit is truth.[9]

When the Second Council of Nicaea, the seventh Ecumenical Council (787), defined the Church's doctrine on the question of images, it appealed to tradition and linked it to the indwelling of the Holy Spirit in the Church.[10] When, in the sixteenth century and especially at the Council of Trent, the value of tradition was justified in the face of the Protestant denials, it was simply a question of returning to the age-old pronouncements, firmly based on the New Testament,

---

[8] See numerous texts and references in EH, pp. 151–66, to which others could be added indefinitely.

[9] AH, 3, 24, 1 (PG 7:966).

[10] Sess. 7 (Denz., 302).

concerning the Holy Spirit as the operating principle of the Mystical Body and the Church's profound principle of identity.[11] The Catholic Church is perfectly aware that she could not attribute the combination of security and authority to tradition as she does, treating it as a norm, if she did not know herself to be assisted by the Holy Spirit, by virtue of our Lord's promise. It is one and the same Spirit, the Spirit of Christ, "who spoke through the prophets" and who established the apostles as witnesses, who is the Church's life force and conscience, the Subject who assures the profound identity of tradition, by which she lives. This same doctrine has been expressed again in modern times by J. A. Möhler (d. 1838) and by the whole theological school of Tübingen, whose leader he was.[12] His entire theory of tradition is that of the life of the Holy Spirit animating the ecclesiastical body ever since Pentecost and ensuring its unity and fellowship throughout time and through the diversity of persons and local communities.

THE CHURCH: VISIBLE AND HISTORICAL SUBJECT OF TRADITION

The Church is a complex organic reality

We use the word "Church" naïvely, thinking that it refers to a simple reality. We should always ask ourselves what exactly it implies. It will be seen that often it refers to the hierarchy, that is, to what the Fathers and St. Thomas Aquinas more correctly called "the leaders of the Church, those who are appointed to preside over the communities, *praepositi*

---

[11] See EH, pp. 219 ff.

[12] See EH, pp. 242 ff.; H. Holstein, *La Tradition dans l'Église*, pp. 118 ff.

Ecclesiae" ("the Church" referring here to the body of the faithful, or of Christians). Indeed, in the writings of the Fathers and in the liturgy, *ecclesia* (Church) means the Christian community, with the pastors or leaders considered first as Christians, that is, as men trying to live by the grace of God and to save their souls. While fully aware of the juridical structure of the Church, the Fathers do not make ecclesiology to consist in defending and illustrating it, as was customary following the controversies of the sixteenth century; the ecclesiology elaborated by them is much more a consideration of the Christian state or way of life within the sacramental and communal framework of the Covenant; it is a Christian anthropology based on the People of God and the Body of Christ, founded respectively on the figurative Pasch of Mount Sinai and the true Pasch of Jerusalem. A phrase often repeated by St. Augustine expresses well the basis of this ecclesiology: "I am a bishop for you, but first a Christian with you, *Vobis sum episcopus, vobiscum christianus.*" The hierarchic aspect is by no means ignored, but it is seen and presented within the context of the Christian life, which remains first and most important.[13] In short, the hierarchic aspect is advanced as an element of an organic reality, intended as such by the Lord.

St. Augustine's fine expression has moreover a poetic value; it is also vigorous. It is in fact a typical feature of St. Augustine's genius to combine imagery and precision, to express a well-constructed and rigorous synthesis in evocative language. There remains only the matter of translating his statement into modern terms and defining it more precisely. A

[13] This view is found in St. Thomas; see ST Ia–IIae, q. 106, a. 1 and 2, which gives the principal lines along which he would have developed an ecclesiology had he developed one explicitly.

reflection that has often been repeated in recent years proves that, with the distinction between personal life and public functions, we are reaching the heart not only of the distinction between hierarchy and laity, but of the differences between the position of the sixteenth-century Reformers and that of the ancient Church. This calls for a brief explanation.

The domain of our personal life corresponds to our personal activity, making use of such faculties as intelligence; culture; physical strength; resources; spiritual gifts of faith, prayer and love; and the energy by which we put all this into practice. We act to our own advantage by living for ourselves. We can act for the benefit of others, even on a fairly large scale, but such activity still remains private by rights, whatever publicity and renown it acquires in fact. Supposing it is a teaching activity, we can communicate our knowledge, or our personal convictions and opinions, to a great number of men, in our own name and on our own initiative. Even if it concerns the apostolate it is the same thing; in this case we are carrying out a mission in the broad sense of this word in the sense that every man is responsible for the gifts he has received, which were bestowed so that he might live by them, certainly, but also so that all the others might profit by them. In this case we may speak of a "mission by responsibility".

The domain of a public activity or function, in the main juridical sense of the word, is something different. It is possible to carry it out using personal resources of intelligence or physical strength, for example, but not in our own name or making use solely of the authority that our gifts or personal worth may give us. It is as though we were clothed with a second personality, and often, as a sign of this, we are materially invested with a uniform or badge of office; we become a public person, endued with a legal authority that transcends our personal merits. I said above that even an activity of great renown remained private since it was carried out in the name of our personal resources. Here, even what we do with the help of our personal resources remains outside the private domain and is counted as part of the public authority. In a teaching activity, we assume the teaching authority of the Church, which goes beyond our own competence, which may be but slender. What about the apostolate? We are not exempt from being zealous or from putting all our zeal at the service of our mission, but we are carrying out a mission in the full, strict sense of the word: a mandate received from a higher authority. A mission is always a certain task demanding resources necessary for its accomplishment. Here, the task is not only the one that we feel we ought to accomplish on account of the personal gifts for which we are responsible; it is the task assigned to us by a Master, who has given us a mandate to this effect and corresponding powers. The mission of the Twelve, passed on subsequently to their successors and then again to others, is one of this sort, "a mission by mandate".

The traditional Catholic view is that our relationship with God is not by nature purely individualistic or personal. The action of widening our personal life to include a certain communication and sharing with others would not be enough to restore the true character of this relationship as intended by God's institution. In short, it is insufficient to correct the personal, individualistic aspect by introducing a communal note. In our relationship with God we should not remain within the framework of a wholly personal and private relationship. In fact, our religious relationship as God intended it, and as he founded it by means of the two successive stages of the Covenant, however personal it is and however much it is directed toward the inner life, is not entirely authentic, left solely to its elements of an individualistic or personal nature. It finds its achievement by passing through a framework established publicly, which is essentially that of the Covenant. We are united to God *personally*, not merely by personal links, by passing through a Church framework that is definitely public, comprising an established ministry, sacraments, etc.

Unless I am mistaken, this is where the line of division between the Protestant Reformation and the ancient Church should be drawn. The Reformation wished to react against a development that was sometimes excessive and often mingled with impure and questionable elements arising from human and fallible interventions. It rejected them and broke free but failed to distinguish between the historical accretions that needed reforming and the divine institution, which should have been respected as such. It replaced a religious relationship that was intrinsically ecclesiastical by one in which the basic elements constituting it were of a purely personal nature; a certain communal note was added subsequently, but it was more of an external addition than an integral part. Each individual formed his own religious relationship by faith in reply to the Word of God, attained by a personal contact with the Bible.

It is time to apply these distinctions to the question of tradition, but the preceding explanations were not unnecessary: having supplied them already, we shall rapidly be able to understand a distinction whose foundations have been laid and that will throw still more light upon what remains to be said about the lay status and the function of the hierarchy.

All Christians are collectively responsible for Christianity, just as, collectively, they all form a holy priesthood and spiritual fabric (cf. 1 Pet 2:5–10). They carry and transmit

Christianity and the Gospel from generation to generation. Within the body of Christians, that is, the Church, the hierarchy, following the apostles, have received the mandate, authority and corresponding power to keep the apostolic deposit and Gospel and to explain them authentically. The mere transmission is one thing: at least in a certain way it concerns everyone; keeping, judging and defining it with the authority of the Magisterium is another: it is the function of the hierarchy, comprising the college of bishops united to the Pope, who is head of this college as Peter was head of the apostolic college. Collectively and organically the faithful and hierarchy form the subject of tradition.

Those readers who have heard of the theory that the Orthodox Christians of Russian origin call *Sobornost*[14] will easily see what it contains that is interesting and profoundly true—and its possibly erroneous and ambiguous implications. This theory consists in developing the role played by the Church in the living conservation of the truth, and opposing a presentation of the facts that makes the hierarchy alone the subject of this conservation, the faithful playing a role that is not only secondary but passive. This would support G. Tyrrell's contention that, according to a certain theology, the Church would be infallible only "because she possesses an infallible pope, rather as a flock of sheep together with their shepherd might be declared intelligent". Within these limits, and in this sense, the *Sobornost* theory of the collegiality or intrinsically conciliar nature of the Church contains a large part of truth and can act as a useful stimulant to make us emphasize an important aspect of the matter that we are in danger of

[14] *Sobornost* is a Russian word signifying "collegiality", collegial system (and therefore conciliar). See the author's *Jalons pour une théologie du laïcat* (Paris, 1954), pp. 380–86 (the passage is omitted from the English translation).

minimizing. It becomes erroneous, on the other hand, even with regard to Eastern and Orthodox tradition, when it is interpreted in such a way as to forget and misconstrue the role, privileges and even existence of the Magisterium of the hierarchy.

The Magisterium of the hierarchy: The chief subject of tradition

The role of the Magisterium is classically defined as keeping faithfully, judging authentically and defining infallibly the content of the deposit.[15]

Its first task is certainly to keep the deposit faithfully. The first function of the Magisterium is one of witness; by the apostolic succession, which is evidently something more than a material continuity sanctioned ritually, the episcopate enters into the unity of mission of which we spoke at the beginning of this chapter and becomes a unique witness-bearer whose unity overcomes the vicissitudes and transience of time, as well as distance and space. The primary duty of those whom the Holy Spirit has established bishops (*episcopos*) or "shepherds" to feed the flock of Christ (Acts 20:28) is to remain steadfast in this position of supra-temporal witness to the Revelation made to the apostles, supremely in Jesus Christ. Peter received the title of rock (*Kepha*) primarily because of his confession of Christ, Son of the Living God (Mt 16:16–19). With him, and after him, this confession is at the heart of the witness borne by the established apostolate to Jesus Christ in accordance with the mission it had received. Every possible "definition" of a

---

[15] First Vatican Council, sess. 3, c. 4 states that "a divine deposit, delivered to the Spouse of Christ, [is] to be kept faithfully and declared infallibly" (Denz. 1800); cf. sess. 4, c. 4 (1836).

particular point of doctrine comes under the Magisterium and is referred to it. Those, therefore, who imagine that the ideal aimed at in exercising the Magisterium is to produce as many gratuitous "definitions" as possible, assigning their elaboration to the theologians, are sadly mistaken. The essential thing is not to define, but to keep the deposit faithfully and to bear witness to its totality by respecting the balance of its different parts. The extreme course of "defining", which the Fathers unanimously consider as a hazardous undertaking, an *ultima ratio*, which it is hoped may be avoided, is resorted to only when necessity decrees that this is the sole way to safeguard the integrity and purity of the apostolic testimony, whose content is the truth of the bond of Covenant sealed in Jesus Christ.

Tradition, in which a whole activity of the Church down the ages has become mingled with the pure transmission of the apostolic heritage, is like a river that carries a little of everything. An English author has compared it to a copious meal with an abundant choice of things to eat and drink. The faithful do not stint themselves in their devotions.[16] Even the Doctors are not sparing in their ideas and theories, and it seems that the greater their genius, the more prolific they are. There is room for classification, to distinguish what is valid from what is not, what is Catholic from what is daring, and the authentic tradition from what carries it, in the historical and purely material sense of the word. It is necessary to distinguish, among the ecclesiastical writers, those who deserve to be called "Fathers" and, among all those who have taught, those who deserve to be called "Doctors". Even

---

[16] Following certain ideas outlined by Newman, J. Guitton has written some interesting and precise reflections on the differences between the order of devotion and that of doctrine. The autonomy of the former with regard to the latter must not, however, be exaggerated.

among those who have been singled out, everything is not of equal value; their writing that bears witness to tradition must be separated from what is quite personal. What, for example, in the Christology or the millennial theories of the second-century writers carries the living faith, and what is obsolete, outdated and unproductive for the future? Is St. Augustine, the Doctor of Grace, a witness of tradition from beginning to end? In short, it is necessary to evaluate the material that tradition provides, and even to judge it, without condemning it. Then only can tradition be of value as a teacher of the present. But it is clear that, without being entirely lacking in judgment, the body of the faithful can neither judge by itself nor reach a judgment that is sufficiently clear, unanimous or capable of imposing itself. The Magisterium alone can do this, since it has a special grace corresponding to the mission entrusted to it.

Its final task is to "define" the traditional belief, where necessary, by promulgating it in the form of a "dogma", that is, a formula that is taken as a norm and is legally binding.[17] The college of bishops united to the Pope as to its head and representing the hierarchy, the Magisterium, or again the "teaching Church", rarely exercises this function. It is not one of its "ordinary" tasks, but is termed "extraordinary", which, according to the Fathers, is exercised only when the Magisterium is forced to do so by the threat to the faith of the Church, brought about by a nascent heresy. It is a fearful obligation. St. Hilary, who suffered exile for resisting an emperor favoring Arianism, was as deeply aware of the difficulty and hazards of any attempt at dogmatic formulation

[17] "Dogma" comes from a root that signifies "to appear", "to seem", hence the meaning "to appear true", "an opinion" (a philosophical opinion, for example). From this the word came to mean a "saying" or "maxim"; in ecclesiastical terminology it is a doctrine that must be believed by the faithful.

as he was of the depth of meaning of the mystery to which
he bore such faithful witness: "We are forced by the blas-
phemous errors of heretics to do what is forbidden: to scale
the heights, to express the ineffable, to dare to touch the
unattainable.... We are forced to imprison indescribable
things within the weakness of our language ... and in expressing it, to surrender to the dangers of the human word what
should have been kept and worshipped in our hearts." [18]
Indeed, the privilege of being able to lay down a law for
belief by formulating a dogma, in the pastoral Magisterium,
is a necessary consequence, but nothing more than a consequence, of its injunction to keep the deposit intact. In certain cases it can safeguard the meaning only by defining the
content and the outlines. This is especially what was done in
the Ecumenical Councils, which were convened when the
Catholic conscience was in doubt over a matter that affected
the whole Church. These Councils have condemned errors,
defined belief and thundered anathemas against those who
persisted in their error.

When the pastoral Magisterium presents its testimony thus
in the form of a "definition" or of dogmatic "canons" when
it promulgates a "dogma", it endows a simple revealed truth,
to which it bears witness, with a *legal* value, binding for the
whole Church. It does this by exercising the *authority* that
it has received to "feed" God's People, by teaching and
governing it. At that precise moment, the pastors of the
Church are more than witnesses, and even more than inter-
preters of the meaning of the deposit; they do not merely
state that those who accept such and such an interpretation
have placed themselves outside the truth and the Church:

---

[18] *De Trinitate*, bk. 2, c. 2 (PL 10:51). See P. A. Liégé, article *Dogme* in the
encyclopedia *Catholicisme* (1952), 3:956–57.

they excommunicate them formally. In this way they exercise their power of ruling or jurisdiction, whose practice,
taken with that of pure testimony and being incorporated
with it—for they are two aspects of the same pastorate—
transforms their testimony into a Church law in matters of
faith, just as there are Church laws in matters of discipline
and worship (canonical power and liturgical power).

By the three activities that we have just explained (keeping, judging and defining), the pastoral Magisterium changes
material tradition, which includes all that one generation
transmits to the next, into rules of belief for the Church (in
the following chapter we shall study the relationship between
tradition and holy Scripture). Indeed, Christians transmit to
other Christians, and even the learned to their colleagues, all
manner of things. What is a historical addition, and what is
really part of the deposit? Above all, what is a personal contribution, and what really belongs to the Church? What is a
personal opinion or the theory of a certain school of thought,
and what expresses the faith of the Church herself? The
deposit alone, the true faith of the Church alone, constitutes
tradition in the sense whereby it imposes itself upon the faithful as the actual content of what they should believe. By the
three acts that we have examined, the pastoral Magisterium
transforms material tradition into formal tradition and, at
least in its major actions, into a rule of faith.

Catholic theology has become increasingly aware of this
since the Council of Trent and Cardinal Bellarmine. During the three centuries that followed them, theology has
taken increasing notice of the role of the Magisterium in
the transformation of material tradition into formal tradition. By this very fact, it has been less concerned with the
transmission effected by the body of the faithful, as such,
turning its attention increasingly to the legal or juridical

aspect of codified tradition. Use of the valuable, but very dangerous, collection by Denzinger-Bannwart has excessively favored modern Catholicism's liking for the juridical approach. I have analyzed elsewhere the process by which a number of theologians have come to identify tradition with the teaching of the Magisterium.[19] During the difficult period of the Modernist crisis, Fr. L. Billot expounded this theology in the most emphatic way by criticizing historicism. He reproached those who distinguished the Magisterium from tradition, and who claimed the latter as at least approaching a rule of faith, with confusing *object* and *rule*. According to him, tradition was indeed the object of faith, but it was only the rule of faith in the act by which the Magisterium transmitted this object with authority, with the result that the rule of faith was really the preaching or active tradition of the Magisterium.

Fr. L. Billot's position by no means compels recognition; in fact, to a disciple of St. Thomas Aquinas it appears untenable. St. Thomas is very familiar with the role of the Church in proposing and, where necessary, defining the faith. With regard to our faith and the position it holds in the present economy, he knows and states that its object or formal motive is uncreated truth, insofar as it is revealed in the holy Scriptures and in the teaching of the Church, which flows from this same uncreated truth.[20] But St. Thomas adds that here the Church is only a secondary rule, measured by the primary rule, which is divine Revelation. She is a sort of echo

---

[19] See EH, pp. 233 ff. Such was not the position of the Magisterium itself; it has always situated itself with reference to Scripture and tradition as to its objective norms, and as having authority only to keep and interpret them authentically. See EH, pp. 257–59.

[20] ST IIa–IIae, q. 5, a. 3, c. and ad 2; *De caritate*, a. 13 ad 6. And cf. ET, chap. 3, n. 87.

or reflection.[21] Upon this Cardinal Cajetan comments: "Note well that God's teaching alone is really the rule of faith. Although the universal Church cannot err in her faith, she is, however, not herself the rule of faith: the divine teaching upon which she is founded alone is." [22] "The Church", he says elsewhere, "is simply *ministra objecti*",[23] simply the means and condition of knowledge of an object which is that of divine Revelation and which, once known, is alone the rule of our adhesion to the faith. The *rule* of faith is inherent to the *object* of faith; the Magisterium is "normative" for the believer in that it transmits the object of faith, that is, the norm. The Church's authority, which proceeds from God and is supported by evidence in Revelation, is exercised in the process of communication coming from God to us, and not in the movement going from us to God, which is the theological impulsion of faith, intrinsically measured by God's Word. The Magisterium is simply the servant, the purveyor of the rule, but it acts by authority coming from God and, when the need arises, makes use of this authority.

It is evident that, in these conditions, the Magisterium enjoys no autonomy with regard to the deposit. There is no moment of its activity as Magisterium—that is, as active tradition—when it is exempt from referring to the deposit and to its statements, since the former is merely a witness to the latter. The spoken word of the apostles was authoritative in exactly the same way as were their writings. The spoken word of the Magisterium derives its authority from, and is related to, apostolic tradition, written or unwritten, taken in its original state, which has been

---

[21] See texts quoted in EH, p. 287, n. 84.
[22] *Commentarium* in IIam–IIae, q. 2, a. 6.
[23] Ibid., q. 1, a. 1, nos. 10 and 12.

perfectly preserved in writing, or in its elaborated, dogmatic state. While it evaluates and judges it, the Magisterium itself depends on tradition, since it is a function within the Church, and not above or outside her, and receives assistance only in keeping and defining the faith *of the Church*. It judges tradition in the sense that it decides whether it is indeed the tradition *of the Church*, but as soon as it has recognized it as such, the Magisterium submits to tradition as to a rule inherent to itself: exactly as the conscience submits to a good as soon as it has discovered it.

This is to say that the Magisterium should take the necessary steps to know and recognize the authentic tradition of the Church. The first step is to look for the mark of unanimity, which has always signified the activity of the Holy Spirit and the presence of God. The rule of St. Vincent of Lérins applies here, described by Fr. d'Alès as "a directing principle for the teaching Church herself". St. Vincent's rule is well known: he said (in 434) that we must believe what has been believed everywhere, always and by everyone, *quod ubique, quod semper, quod ab omnibus*.[24] We shall doubtless have occasion to return to this "canon" or rule to examine its excessively static, not to say archaizing, character, and thus its limited validity. It is useful at least in the realm of *positive* application in the sense that what has been held everywhere, always and by everyone belongs definitely to the Church's tradition—and this is what interests us here.

The second step is to study and refer to those competent in the subject of the monuments of tradition. The need for this step is related to the fact that the grace promised to the Magisterium is not one of *inspiration*, but of *assistance*. It is not a gift of invention, but of discernment. The Magisterium does

[24] *Commonitorium*, c. 2 (PL 50:639).

not enjoy infused knowledge; it has first to search for the meaning of the texts, to question the monuments that have come down to us, about the beliefs and faith of our Fathers, and see in what way decisions already made shape doctrine. Naturally the Magisterium can do this unaided, but often it does not possess the means and turns to experts for help. Their opinion is regarded by the Magisterium neither as binding nor as restrictive in any way: it judges it from above. But, on the other hand, the God of Revelation does not contradict the God of science. Nothing escapes the evidence of the facts (shades of Galileo!). It is evident that, without being part of the teaching Church in the dogmatic sense of this expression, the theologians nonetheless have a supporting role to play.

The faithful

With regard to the faithful, I should like to answer two questions here: What activities make them subjects of active tradition? And in this respect, what is their relationship with the pastoral Magisterium: Do they add something to it?

As simple believers we keep and transmit tradition primarily by the acts and gestures of our practice of the Christian faith, which reveals our communion in the faith of the whole Church and of the generations that have preceded us, right back to the apostles. St. Thomas Aquinas speaks of unwritten apostolic traditions preserved in the Church's practice and transmitted as such from one baptized person to another, *per successionem fidelium.*[25]

Do not imagine a special initiation ceremony or anything esoteric, but simply the practice of the Christian faith day in

[25] ST IIIa, q. 25, a. 3 ad 4.

and day out, through the years until death. The faith is received by the newly baptized baby together with life, and with the nourishment and warmth of his home. Our catechetics and sacraments rarely produce fruits that are durable where they have not grown in the atmosphere of the home. It is the Christian parents, much more than priests and preachers, who really transmit the faith. They do it, above all, in the intimate and vital way that I have compared to upbringing as opposed to instruction. The daily example given right up to death, which is the supreme example; the way in which topics are discussed and events judged; the prayer and humble, familiar gestures of the liturgy, which Fr. Doncœur has proposed as the elements of a "return to Christianity"; and finally, in due time, an explicit religious teaching: all these are humble but efficacious means of transmitting the Gospel—sometimes without the action of the hierarchy and priests, as history has more than once testified. The Gospel has been brought to entire regions, at first simply by the faithful: to Georgia, Abyssinia, etc. An Indian race in South America kept the faith without priests for more than eighty years; so did the Japanese Christians from the beginning of the seventeenth century to 1864, when the first missionary was able to return to Nagasaki. Under Turkish domination in Hungary in the seventeenth century, under the French Revolution, and today in the popular democracies, the Catholic faith and Christianity have been transmitted, in great part, by the faithful.

Much has been said these last few years about bearing witness: bearing witness by our life, which is the most incontrovertible sign of the Gospel; bearing witness by the spoken word, which is indispensable to explain the sign of the Gospel and to announce Jesus Christ fully. And we must add witness by the practice of Christianity, by the liturgy and feasts, which testify to the mysteries of salvation and establish us as witnesses simply by our participation.

These means of transmission possess the particular characteristic of saying much more than is actually expressed and of including the integral message, over and above what is consciously held. For the practice of the faith contains the whole of it, as long as nothing is intentionally excluded; this has been mentioned above, and a very fine passage on the subject by M. Blondel was quoted. Symbolism lends itself well to the expression of this totality, aimed at by the practice of the faith. The whole of military discipline is contained in the command "Attention!" and the whole of patriotism in the saluting of the colors. The whole of Christianity is contained in a sign of the cross; no theory of the Redemption expresses half as much as a simple crucifix hung on a wall, erected as a wayside shrine or put on a tomb or altar. A symbol contains a possibility of total communion, and its faithful repetition expresses something that escapes all conceptual analysis. This is why mere believers can transmit the whole of tradition even when they are quite ignorant of the terminology and subtleties of dogma.

It is obvious, however, that this ignorance needs the learning of the Doctors and that this fidelity itself needs the active tradition of the Magisterium, exercising the functions that I have mentioned.

It must be noted first of all that the fidelity of simple believers is exercised on a Christian faith that they have received, which has been preached and communicated to them by means of catechetics and the administration of the sacraments. It is radically dependent on the apostolic mission, in the strict sense, and on the organism willed by God to realize it. "But how are men to call upon him [the Lord] in whom they have not believed? And how are they to believe in him of whom they have never heard? And how are they to hear without a preacher? And how can men preach unless they are sent?" (Rom 10:14–15a). The fidelity of simple believers is radically dependent on the active tradition of the established Magisterium: the flock has pastors to feed it and "supervisors" (*episcopos*) to watch over it. The story of the Japanese Christians, its positive and even stirring aspect that I mentioned, has also a negative aspect: a whole section of them lapsed into a regrettable form of syncretism, and their descendants continued to perpetuate their error. We are familiar with the sorrowful judgment of the Curé d'Ars: "Leave a village without a priest for twenty years and they will worship animals!"

If the faithful are thus dependent on the pastoral Magisterium, in the witness they bear they simply send it back an echo of its own teaching. This is why certain writers have *reduced* their testimony entirely to that of the hierarchy. Fr. A. Goupil writes, for instance: "The passive infallibility of the faithful consists in correctly obeying the Magisterium." [26] This is going too far. First, because it has happened that, although the local Magisterium, the only one to which the faithful had access, remained silent or made an error at that particular time, the faithful remained loyal to the true faith. Newman has studied one phase in the Arian crisis from this point of view. During this crisis it happened that the laity, further removed from the political and imperial complications, were more faithful to what they had received from their pastors. It is to facts of this kind that St. Hilary of Poitiers refers when he writes: "The ears of the faithful are holier than the hearts of the bishops." [27]

[26] *La Règle de la Foi*, no. 17, 2d ed. (Paris, 1941), p. 48.
[27] *Contra Auxentium*, no. 6 (PL 10:613).

It is true then that, even in critical cases of which there are a few instances, the laity echoes the Magisterium's own teaching. All Catholic theologians agree on this, but it is a minimum with which several, among whom I place myself, are not satisfied. In fact this echo is not automatic: it is emitted by living subjects and as such cannot fail to contribute something original. There are *two* testimonies and not merely *one* testimony with its echo. The somewhat professional testimony of the Magisterium is supported by one of another sort, a little as the professional apostolate of the priest is complemented by the apostolate of the layman, so authentic in its naïvety. Newman said that in this way there was a "conspiracy" of priests and faithful, that is, an active cooperation resulting in something wider and richer.

It may be added that if the whole tradition of the Church cannot be reduced to the mechanical transmission of inert objects, since it is carried by a living subject and knows a development, so the Magisterium and Doctors are not alone in achieving this growth in the Church's conscience, as we shall see in the next chapter. The faithful make a very large contribution. They do this by their piety and the exercise of their religious life; it is a fact that they have made a forceful contribution to the development of the Church's belief concerning the mystery of Mary, for instance. This has been shown for the dogma of the Immaculate Conception. But they also do it by a scientific study of the sources of the faith and of the monuments of tradition, by philosophical and even theological reflection, by artistic and cultural creations that concern religion, and by apostolic and missionary efforts, without counting all that monks and spiritual men who were not priests have contributed to the treasury of Christian spirituality. All this shows that there is a very considerable lay contribution to a transmission that is also a development, since it is living. It is impossible for such a profound reality to be simply accidental and not the fulfillment of an integral aspect of the nature of things.

Living tradition: The Catholic spirit

Much has been said about living tradition since the Catholic theologians of Tübingen who, though they did not coin the expression, assured it a brilliant future. It is a fine expression, but it can include things that are quite different. For those who first created it, in the setting of the discussion over the Five Jansenist Propositions, it referred basically to the *present* teaching of the Magisterium: for the Jansenists were fond of referring to tradition but objected to the judgment of the Pope on the Five Propositions, or at least so far as they were attributed to Jansenius. It is equally in this sense that the expression is used by many contemporary theologians who stress the role of the Magisterium, and in certain texts of Pius XII. For Möhler and the Catholic theologians of Tübingen, "living tradition" meant either a conviction expressed in all its breadth by one's entire way of life, with emphasis placed on life in a community,[28] or, more simply, the growth through time of the truth entrusted to the Church, like the growth of a living plant.[29] It is this latter interpretation that is the more adequate. Tradition is living because it is carried by living minds—minds living in time. These minds meet with problems or acquire resources, in time, which lead them to endow tradition, or the truth it contains, with the reactions and characteristics of a living thing: adaptation, reaction, growth and fruitfulness. Tradition is living because it

[28] Thus in J. Sailer and above all Möhler.
[29] Thus in Gugler, Drey and J. E. von Kuhn.

resides in minds that live by it, in a history that comprises activity, problems, doubts, opposition, new contributions and questions that need answering.

Another expression recurs frequently, in forms that are closely linked: the Catholic spirit, *sensus catholicus*; the spirit of the faith, *sensus fidei*; the ecclesiastical spirit, *phronèma ekklèsiastikon*; the mind of the Church, *Ecclesiae catholicae sensus*, or sometimes *consensus Ecclesiae*.[30] Today we often use similar terms: "Catholic spirit" and "mind of the Church". By this is meant a disposition having the Church as its object, or reference at least, and which is composed above all of respect and docility. Here the word "Church" primarily connotes the idea of the hierarchic Magisterium and even of the Roman Magisterium. Such was not exactly the original meaning of our expressions. *Ecclesia*, "Church" in the writings of the Fathers and the liturgical texts (it would be useful to read in the Missal the fine Lenten Collects, for example, and those generally through the liturgical year), signifies almost exactly what we call the Christian community or the community of Christians, referring equally well to the local community actually assembled as to the universal community of all those who belong to Jesus Christ within his Covenant. In addition, in the ancient texts and again at the Council of Trent, which used these expressions very frequently, the words "spirit" and "faith" did not describe so much the subjective disposition as the objective content, *what* the Church believes. Once again the rule is incorporated in the object. Tradition is what the ecclesiastical community believes, under its pastors, and is guaranteed by the Holy Spirit, who resides and operates in it. "And we are witnesses to these things,

---

[30] References will be found in chapter 3 of ET. The expression *phronèma ekklèsiastikon* is by Hippolytus, in Eusebius' HE, 5, 28, 6. It is referred to by Newman, Möhler, Passaglia and Franzelin.

and so is the Holy Spirit whom God has given to those who obey him" (Acts 5:32; cf. Jn 15:26–27). However, if this rule exists in written documents—Creed, canons of Councils, writings of the Fathers, the liturgy—it is alive in the Church, inseparable from the *ecclesia*, its living subject. From this point of view the objective meaning of the expressions *sensus fidei, sensus catholicus, sensus Ecclesiae* already signifies for the Fathers an interior disposition experienced within the fellowship of the Church—a sort of instinct or inner feeling.

Modern theology has principally followed this trend of subjective dispositions. Möhler followed the Fathers too closely to avoid confusing the two aspects, as they had done. He wrote in his famous *Symbolik*, for example: "The Spirit of God, who governs and animates the Church, produces an instinct in man, a form of Christian intuition that leads him to the true doctrine"; "this inner feeling, this conscience, is tradition, a chain of reflection and testimony that may be traced back from century to century, right to the divine Master".[31] And yet Möhler compared the Catholic spirit to the genius of a people, or a national spirit, *Volksgeist*; a living link between the past and the present, this spirit is embodied and realized objectively in laws and institutions, and supremely in the state. Such is tradition: the community spirit whose profound inner force is the Pentecostal Spirit and that lives, is transmitted within the ecclesiastical fellowship and is expressed in the monuments of the Church's faith.

Already Möhler and his disciples,[32] followed by Newman and, after them, a great number of contemporary theologians, speak readily of the spirit of the faith (*sensus fidei Ecclesiae*) in terms of "awareness". Tradition is here envisaged as

---

[31] *Symbolik*, 38.
[32] Staudenmeier and A. Tanner (1862), for example.

the Church's awareness, comprising the subjective and objective aspects already mentioned, respectively as act, or faculty, and as content. In this view its role in the Church would be similar to that played by awareness in a person's life: comprehension and memory, gauge of identity, instinct of what is fitting, witness and expression of personality. In fact, it is a happy analogy that can tell us much. It must be noted, however, that without actually excluding it, the idea of awareness does not in itself express an essential aspect of tradition, namely, the fact that it is received as data, as a deposit. The Church does not only possess self-awareness; she keeps and actualizes the living memory of what she has received, and whose presence and vigor her Beloved Lord continually sustains within her. In a sense, this awareness possesses its object integrally from the start, but it does not express it fully at each moment.

Newman has made a good analysis of this real possession, not simply of a vital instinct even, but of definite ideas and convictions, which we may carry within us subconsciously, without expressing them clearly or explicitly. What we received in our early formation, which is scarcely instruction but almost pure "upbringing", and which is like the very life formed in the maternal womb, is a particularly good example of this. And we know that it corresponds fairly exactly to tradition.

The Fathers and the Councils never separate the subjective instinct of the faith from the objective content received from preceding generations. For them there is no question of autonomy for the subjective, mystical instinct of spiritual things, concerning the proposition that God has himself made us, according to all the means he has established to this end, forming as it were a scale of descending importance: the Revelation made to the prophets and apostles, the Church, the

Councils, the Fathers, the Doctors and the saints. Certain modern theories, which I have criticized elsewhere, do not pay enough respect to this balance and, overstressing the aspect of "Church" or "Magisterium", come to attribute to them a sort of autonomy with regard to the deposit, whose content can be obtained only in the objective monuments. The Magisterium does not have an autonomous value: it receives assistance only when it keeps, interprets and defines the *Revelation*, of which it has been made a witness. Similarly, the Church has no power to create truth. This is why the subjective instinct of the faith should always seek expression in the objective setting of the truths, customs, rites and behavior on which the Church agrees, and in the fellowship in space as well as time, which, in its Councils, has always borne witness, using such terms as "This is what the Church believes, this is what she has always believed; it is what we have received from our Fathers and what we have lived by, faithful to their traditions".

CHAPTER III

THE CONTENT OF TRADITION:
TRADITION AND SCRIPTURE

I have already quoted the decree of the Council of Trent of April 8, 1546 (Denz. 783); it places its statements concerning the canonical Scriptures and the apostolic traditions under the authority of the Gospel. What the Council considers to be at issue is the purity and totality of the Gospel. *Its purity*: the aim of the Council in general, and of the decree it puts forward in particular, is to clear away the errors in order that the purity of the Gospel may be safeguarded, *ut sublatis erroribus puritas ipsa Evangelii in Ecclesia conservetur. Its totality*: this refers to the fact that the Gospel content, in the form of truths and rules of behavior, is not limited to the Scriptures alone, but is also contained in books *and* unwritten traditions. The Carmelite Thomas Netter had already reproached Wyclif that by his almost exclusive recourse to the Bible, he cut the heritage in half and kept only half of the Christian faith transmitted by the apostles.[1] Similarly, the Council sees the traditions against an apostolic background and the respecting of these traditions as a condition of our fidelity to the totality of the apostles' heritage. To keep the writings alone

---

[1] *Doctrinale Antiquitatum fidei*, praef. lib. 1, a. 2, chap. 23 (Venice, 1571).

would mean keeping only part of this heritage, for the apostles have left us more than this.

The content of tradition, which is the subject of this chapter, is related therefore to the Gospel. This notion of *the Gospel* has been carefully studied from the aspects of the scriptural texts, but unfortunately it has been neglected in the tradition of the Church—the Fathers, the liturgy, the monuments and medieval theology. In these, the emphasis appears to be especially on the following typical features of "the Gospel": it is not a means among others, but the source; and it is the source because it presents Jesus Christ, not only by announcing him but by showing him as present and active for the purpose of our salvation. It does not merely represent a form of knowledge, but an active force, exactly like the Word of God: "It is the power of God for salvation to every one who has faith" (Rom 1:16). Jesus Christ operates not only in and through the sacraments, but also in and through the proclamation of salvation, considered by tradition as an advent of the saving Word.

So, whether we consider tradition as a way other than Scripture of transmitting the saving deposit or as containing something not strictly found in the Scriptures, it appears immediately as bringing nothing other than *the Gospel*, that is, the knowledge and virtue of Jesus Christ, Son of God and Savior. In tradition it is merely a question of the purity and totality of the religious bond of the Covenant fulfilled in Jesus Christ. I shall go no further in this chapter, but I should like to develop two points especially that lie at the very heart of our subject: the relationship between Scripture and tradition; and the aspect of duration in history and, consequently, the aspects of comprehensiveness and development essential to tradition.

SCRIPTURE AND TRADITION

The earliest Fathers, up to St. Theophilus of Antioch, St. Irenaeus and St. Hippolytus, that is, up to the beginning of the third century, generally understood by "Scripture" the writings of the Old Testament. The tradition they distinguish from Scripture contains the authentic interpretation of Scripture, according to God's plan and within its framework. St. Irenaeus compares heretics to those who produce a picture of a dog or fox in a mosaic of colored blocks when asked to portray a king, or again to those who compose poems by plagiarizing lines from *The Iliad*.[2] They make use of texts, but since they do not read them within the Church, they do not read them according to the tradition of the apostles.

This tradition of the apostles was their preaching itself, which consisted in proclaiming Christ according to the Scriptures and showing Christ to be the fulfillment of the Scriptures and the center from which they take their meaning. When, on the road to Emmaus, Christ accompanied the two disillusioned and discouraged disciples, who were discussing the collapse of their hopes as irrevocable, he rebuked them in these terms: "'O foolish men, and slow of heart to believe all that the prophets have spoken!' ... And beginning with Moses and all the prophets, he interpreted to them in all the scriptures concerning himself" (Lk 24:25–27). Soon afterward, when Jesus had rejoined the apostles in the Upper Room, he told them: "'These are my words which I spoke to you, while I was still with you, that everything written about me in the law of Moses and the prophets and the psalms must be fulfilled.' Then he opened their minds to

---

[2] AH, I, 8, I and 9, 4 (PG 7:521, 544 ff.; Harvey, I, pp. 67–68, 86–87).

understand the scriptures, and said to them, 'Thus it is written. . . . You are witnesses of these things'" (Lk 24:44–48).

The evangelist Philip had met a eunuch, a courtier of Candace, queen of Ethiopia, on the road from Jerusalem to Gaza; the eunuch was reading the prophet Isaiah and wondering to whom these words of the prophet referred: "As a sheep led to the slaughter . . . so he opens not his mouth." When Philip asked him if he understood what he was reading, the eunuch replied: "How can I, unless someone guides me?" (Acts 8:31). Then Philip explained it to him. But, as Bellarmine has already remarked,[3] he did not give him a lesson in Hebrew, nor did he translate the passage, just as Jesus had not given the apostles, who knew it, a Hebrew lesson. Just as Jesus had done with the apostles, Philip preached to him about Jesus, taking this passage as his theme. To give the meaning of Scripture is to explain it in the light of God's plan, whose focal point is Jesus Christ. The modern studies on the apostolic "kerygma" (the preaching of Christ and of the saving Gospel), those that have shown that our Gospels were a means of teaching about Christ, that they aimed at presenting the historical Christ from a certain number of accounts and showing that the prophetic predictions had found their fulfillment in him— all these studies prove that the apostles' preaching and tradition did in fact consist in revealing the entire structure of the economy of salvation, in relation to Christ, as to its center, around whom all the rest was arranged, shaped and took its meaning.

Thus the apostles simply continued a method of presentation inaugurated by Jesus himself.[4] If their doctrinal tradition

---

[3] *Controversae, De Verbo Dei*, lib. 3, c. 1 (*Opera* [Paris, 1870], 1:167).

[4] See EH, p. 78 f., and the references on pp. 114–15, nn. 4 and 5. Also G. A. F. Knight, *A Christian Theology of the Old Testament* (London, 1959).

consists in understanding Scripture in the light of Christ and
the Church, that is, the Christian mystery, it must be admitted
as being a tradition not merely apostolic in origin, but divine,
since, having founded it, Jesus communicated it to them by sup-
plying them with the key to the Scriptures.

This was the principal interpretation given by the early
Fathers to apostolic tradition. Irenaeus gives "the expound-
ing of the Scriptures" as its equivalent. "The object of ecclesiastical tradition [for him] was to repeat and transmit the
preaching by which the apostles have announced, since the
Old Testament, that Christ was the end of the divine plan
and the fulfilment of all the prophecies, to such an extent
that for the bishop of Lyons, the *paradosis* is identified with
the *kerygma ton apostolon*". This ecclesiastical and traditional
understanding of the Scriptures represents the true "gnosis".
Following St. Paul, the Fathers understand by this a spiritual
gift whose object or content is the knowledge of God's ways,
the key to the important saving acts accomplished by Christ
and to their proclamation in Scripture. Tradition and "gnosis" are correlative, like the means and result. Both come
from the Holy Spirit; both depend on the life in the Church,
which is the receptacle of the gifts of the Holy Spirit: according to St. Irenaeus, she is like a precious vase to which the
Spirit ceaselessly communicates an overflowing spirit of youth
as well as rejuvenates the deposit it contains.[5]

The Fathers, who had to combat heresies, are unanimous
in asserting that this true understanding of the Scriptures is
found only in the Church. And since it is the principal element of tradition for them, they include the whole of tradition within this notion. We find and hold it, according to
them, only in the Church. Their statements to this effect are

[5] AH, 3, 24, 1 (PG 7:966; Harvey, 2, p. 131).

so numerous that they would fill a whole chapter. Origen
writes, for example: "The true disciple of Jesus is he who
enters the house, that is to say, the Church. He enters it by
thinking as the Church does and living as she does; this is
how he understands her Word. The key to the Scriptures
must be received from the tradition of the Church, as from
the Lord himself."[6] Summing up the position of St. Irenaeus by quoting many of his writings, Fr. Van den Eynde
adds his own testimony by saying:

> We must interpret the Scriptures according to the tradition pre-
> served in the Church. When we know the subject treated by
> Homer, says St. Irenaeus, we can distinguish his poems from
> the imitations. Similarly, when "we possess the unchanging
> canon of truth, received at baptism", we no longer discover
> heretical theories in the terms, expressions and parables of Scrip-
> ture, but we easily adjust all the texts to the body of truth. . . .
> The Church is like a paradise planted in this world. We must
> seek nourishment in this paradise, from its trees; we must read
> the sacred books in the Church. . . . The spiritual man must read
> the Scriptures "near to the presbyters who possess the apos-
> tolic doctrine" in order to find an interpretation that is cor-
> rect, harmonious and free from danger and blasphemy.[7]

The Church alone is the place where truth is assured—
the Church, that is, the community of Christians, as was said
above, but especially, within the community, the Magisterium transmitted by apostolic succession: "It is the presbyters
who preserve our faith in a single God, Creator of everything; they who increase our love for the Son of God, Author

[6] See further quotations from the Fathers in EH, pp. 48–49 and corresponding notes, pp. 100–101.

[7] *Les normes de l'enseignement chrétien dans la littérature patristique des trois pre-
miers siècles* (Paris: Gembloux, 1933), pp. 268–69.

of the economy of salvation; who explain the Scriptures to us without danger, without blaspheming God, without dishonoring the patriarchs, and without despising the prophets." [8] Tertullian has expressed these ideas rigorously in a well-known juridical formula. The Church, he said, is a proprietor: she owns the Scriptures. By what right do heretics seize them and betray their meaning? [9]

It has been the unanimous and constant tradition of the Church to read the Scriptures with reference to Christ and to the Christian mystery. It is also the tradition of the liturgy, which is thus the inmost nucleus of tradition and would be sufficient in itself to teach the whole of Christianity, as is shown by the example of the Eastern Christians. It was also the tradition of the Fathers of the classical age. Whether it be in their treatises against heresy or in their pastoral activity and preaching, they simply expound the Scriptures and use them to illustrate the Christian mystery, to which they continually return, whatever the subject under discussion. Such, finally, was the tradition of the whole of the Middle Ages, in which men were also steeped in the Bible. Writers of that time brought a greater profusion to their commentaries and sometimes fell into an exaggerated use of symbolism and allegory. But the basis of their exegesis, as Fr. Henri de Lubac has shown with a finesse and erudition difficult to excel, was exactly the same as that of the exegesis of the Fathers and the liturgy: it was centered on Christ and the Church and aimed at explaining the Christian mystery. What has been thus unanimously "traditional" for fifteen centuries and is derived manifestly, not only from the apostles but from the Lord himself, cannot cease to be traditional today. The whole of her past

---

[8] AH, 4, 36, 5.
[9] See his *Treatise of Prescription against Heretics*, chaps. 7, 15, 17.

compels the Church to believe that her *dogmatic* tradition is related to the Scriptures and consists in transmitting the sense of the Scriptures, taken as a whole. This does not imply that the *whole* of tradition is reduced to this or that in its doctrinal content it is *only* an exegetical tradition. It implies that this is its essence.

Knowing that the content or object of dogmatic tradition is closely linked to Scripture, since it represents the latter's range of experience from the ecclesiastical and corporate to the apostolic, let us attempt to define this relationship more precisely. For this I shall use the fundamental distinction I made in the first chapter, in considering tradition either as a *means other* than Scripture in communicating Christianity or as having a *content other* than the holy Scriptures. In both cases tradition is not Scripture; it is something else, in the widest sense. But in the first case, it presents or can present the same content in a different way—and this "other way" will need defining exactly; in the second case, it presents a content not given by the Scriptures.

Tradition as an original and different means

For the Fathers, tradition presents first the content of the Scriptures, which contain in one way or another all that is necessary to live as God wishes us to (the details of which will be given later), and it interprets the meaning of the Scriptures. In fact, this meaning is not given clearly by Scripture itself and is found, in a certain way, outside it.

To understand this fully, it would be necessary to develop the traditional conception of how the sacred texts should be read for a true perception and enjoyment of God's Word. The divine Scriptures are regarded as a kind of sacrament: a grace-bearing sign that effectively realizes communion with

God, and salvation, when it is used in the right conditions. These conditions are obviously spiritual: humility, purity of heart, a true desire to seek God and a strong love of the Gospel; but this spiritual approach is not of a psychological or moral order that is purely individualistic: it requires that we place ourselves in God's plan, in the framework of his Covenant, in the perspective of the communication he himself wishes to make to us, that is, in the fellowship of his People. The Scriptures do not surrender their meaning by the bare text; they surrender it to a mind that is living, and living in the conditions of the Covenant. This mind, or living subject, is the one we studied in the last chapter; it is the Church, God's People, the Body of Christ and Temple of the Holy Spirit. Thus, in a certain way, Scripture possesses its meaning outside itself. In the categories of the Scholastic analysis of the sacraments, it would be termed the fruit of Scripture, its *res* (the spiritual reality resulting from the sacrament). The reality contained in the sacred text would be described as its literary, historical or exegetical meaning, but its dogmatic meaning is found outside the text, considered materially, which supposes the intervention of a new activity, namely, the faith of the Church. The place where this is found is precisely tradition as it is understood by the early Fathers; it is there, in this setting and in these conditions, that the holy Scriptures reveal their meaning—a meaning that is not simply the one accessible to philologists and historians but that which must nourish God's People in order that it may be God's People in the fullest sense.[10] It may be

[10] The vicious circle here is only apparent. It appears, indeed, that the Bible must be incorporated into the faith of God's People in order to produce the whole of its meaning as God's Word, whereas this Word of God is part of, or at least a shaping influence of, God's People. This is true; and it supposes that "God's People", or the Church, exists in two phases: one where she is, as it

noted that what I have said here corresponds exactly to what Maurice Blondel had rediscovered, starting from his reflection as a Christian philosopher, independently of an authentically or technically theological analysis.

The doctrine that has just been presented is that of all the Fathers of the Catholic tradition, as much in the East as in the West. It is denied in the Protestant theory of the sufficiency of Scripture, expounded systematically in the Protestant orthodoxy of the beginning of the seventeenth century. According to this theory, Scripture possesses by itself and in itself, that is, without needing the addition of any other principle, the qualities of a real sacrament of salvation, or rather, of saving faith. It possesses authority, making it recognized and developing it unaided; it possesses efficacy, being the principal—and for some the sole—means of grace; it contains all that is necessary for the Christian; it is clear, explaining itself without help and needing nothing besides itself to make known God's thoughts. But a contemporary Dutch Protestant writer has said: "Was the

---

were, responsible for her own existence, her own begetter, and another where she is simply begotten: *Ecclesia congregans* and *Ecclesia congregata*. The first phase is that of the apostles, who believed directly in Christ. They "received the Word" into their faith, which they themselves expressed in their writings and delivered in their tradition. It is starting from this tradition, and by receiving it, that the Church can establish herself upon God's Word and feed upon it to become God's People fully. After the apostles, in fact, God chose and raised up men who, in a lesser and secondary though still real way, played a similar part; those whom we call the "Fathers" are precisely the first men whose faith, lived in the sight of the whole Church, was in some way a foundation and mold of the Church's faith, which they transmitted to her in a "tradition" that allowed her to receive more fully the words of Revelation by which she lives as God's People. It is in this way, for example, that the Church's trinitarian belief is passed on by St. Athanasius, at one remove from the apostles, or, concerning especially the divinity of the Holy Spirit, by St. Basil and the Cappadocian Fathers.

motto of the Reformation not *Scripture alone?* On the contrary, the plurality of Churches belies this motto." [11]

The theory of the sufficiency of Scripture to reveal its meaning as that of the Word, by which God wishes his people to live in his Covenant, encounters the difficulty of differences of interpretation. This situation is not a new one, but perhaps Protestants have hesitated to draw conclusions from it because it was imprudently exploited by Catholic controversialists. Today, Protestants themselves are rediscovering it in the setting and climate of ecumenism. Gathered round God's Word contained in Scripture, they are aware of the profound unity it communicates to them—the unity, in fact, of Christianity—and owing to the fact that they are different and possess different doctrinal systems, at the same time they realize, for this very reason, that each has read holy Scripture following a certain tradition. The unity itself that exists between them comes from the Bible, whose text they hold in common, but not from the Bible alone: it comes also from what the Reformers retained of the tradition of the ancient Church, judging it consonant with Scripture and basing it especially on the Apostles' Creed, the first four Ecumenical Councils, and even partly on the Fathers, whom they are at present rediscovering in a way that is quite remarkable.

They have also been rediscovering the Church for about a generation now, at least in her communal aspect, if not yet in that aspect revealing her as a public institution of divine right and an organically structured body. This discovery is leading an increasing number of Protestant theologians to realize that the Scriptures, a book given to God's People, can be understood in its fullest and purest sense only if it is read

[11] J. N. Bakhuisen van den Brink, "La Tradition dans l'Église primitive et au XVIème siècle", *Revue d'Hist. et de Philos. Relig.* 36 (1956): 271.

in the Church, in the fellowship of the entire People of God. More and more remarkable statements to this effect are being made. I am very glad that this is so, without, however, being ignorant of the still considerable distance separating them from traditional Catholic doctrine. Here are one or two of these statements:

> Protestants must in their turn agree that Rome is right to insist that holy Scripture is the Church's book and can only be really understood in the midst of God's People.... We must learn afresh the value of a communal reading of Scripture: it is within the family raised up by scriptural Revelation that the sacred writings assume their full meaning.[12]

> Much research remains to be done on the witness borne by the Holy Spirit to the Church. This task is all the more urgent since we have not finished ridding ourselves of our Protestant individualism. If the Spirit gives to each believer the certainty that Christian witness is truly God's Word and that he is saved in Jesus Christ, this witness and this certainty are only given to him and renewed if he lives within the fellowship of the Church. It is a fact experienced by everyone that the Spirit only permits us to see a few pages of the Bible simultaneously, and that we must discover and even constantly rediscover the others. Theology is equally the concern of all the members of Christ's body.[13]

Tradition is thus a universal and ecumenical reading of Scripture by the Church in the light of the Holy Spirit. This ecclesiastical reading alone will lead us to the fullness of God's Word. It is true that a theologian, an exegete or a historian may possess particular talents for the interpretation of a text.

[12] R. M. Achard, "Écriture et Tradition dans le dialogue entre les chrétiens séparés", in *Réforme*, February 2, 1957.

[13] Théo Preiss, *Le Témoignage intérieur du Saint-Esprit*, p. 36, n. 2.

But these talents are only efficacious when placed in the understanding of the whole Church, guided by the Holy Spirit. This implies the need to place exegesis and theology in tradition and in the present-day ecumenical activity, since a complete understanding of Scripture depends upon a reading that is not only historical, but traditional and ecumenical.[14]

Other quotations could be added to these, and others will be found in my *Essai théologique* (chap. 7). However incomplete it may still be, the truth expressed in such texts corroborates the Catholic conviction that Scripture can be read authentically only in the Church and according to tradition. It was this conviction that motivated the Church's vigorous reaction when, at the beginning of the nineteenth century, biblical societies undertook a massive dissemination of the sacred text in every language, under the naïve impression that the literal text of the holy Scriptures, as such and by itself, was sufficient to produce truth and salvation. It is easy to understand how much the decrees condemning this practice must appear scandalous to sincere Protestants who, on the one hand, profess a religious veneration for the Bible and, on the other, have no idea, either of the historical context of these measures[15] or of the style peculiar to certain ecclesiastical documents.[16] The biblical societies have become

---

[14] M. Thurian, *L'Unité visible des chrétiens et la Tradition* (Taizé, 1961), pp. 11–12.

[15] That, in particular, of a veritable onslaught against the Catholic Church, which was threatened, at the beginning of the nineteenth century, on one side by Protestant societies with a pronounced purpose of proselytism, and on the other by the rationalist societies (Freemasonry, the Carbonari, and so forth); and this was at a moment when the Catholic Church, greatly weakened by the French Revolution and its aftermath, was in a defensive position.

[16] Such expressions come to mind as "a deadly spring dispensing poison", "perverse machinations" (Pius VII, Sept. 8, 1816); "plague", "poisonous pastures" (Leo XII, May 5, 1824). Besides biblical allusions, they spring from the special medieval style used in decrying heresy: this style deserves a study.

wiser without lessening their activity. The Catholic Church is cured of the siege mentality she has known at times; she has regained the initiative with increasing determination, even in the biblical field. This is why the condemnations of biblical societies no longer appear in the collection of Roman decisions on biblical questions, namely, the *Enchiridion Biblicum*. And yet, the basic principles that profoundly inspired the protestations and transcended the dated form they took are still valid. They derive from the truth I am developing here, that is, the fact that the material book called "The Holy Bible", which can be bought as such at any bookseller's, is only the true Bread of Life for God's People when it is interpreted correctly, according to the meaning implanted in it by God, and that this is possible only in the Church, in and by her tradition.

In concrete terms, this requirement is expressed primarily by certain external conditions: that the translation be judged faithful by the pastoral Magisterium (imprimatur) and that it be accompanied by notes: not merely by cross-references, however precious this system is (those in the edition produced by the Biblical Society are excellent), but by notes that add a scientific and exegetical value to a theological one of explanations consonant with tradition. But it is well to note that these external conditions are not in themselves a complete program for studying holy Scripture in the living tradition of the Church—far from it! A mere observance of the letter does not satisfy the spirit.

One of the greatest advantages of reading the holy Scriptures in the Church is the synthesis obtained. The more one studies the Fathers and learns about the liturgy, the more one admires their skill in putting the scriptural texts together, not from a merely literary point of view, as the exegetes do—which is very valuable in its own sphere—but going beyond the literal sense, sometimes even in a way that is quite disconcerting from an exegetical point of view, and relating these texts to the inner *reality* underlying the entire Scriptures, on a final analysis, the relationship of Covenant, the Christian mystery. The fact is that the Fathers and the liturgy are, above all, witnesses of the synthesis and meaning of Christian reality, which is also the supreme realm of tradition. One of the difficulties of reading the holy Scriptures is that they do not present this synthesis explicitly. They comprise forty-six writings for the Old Testament [thirty-nine in a Protestant Bible], of which certain are composed of several documents, and twenty-seven writings for the New Testament, the entire collection representing the greatest diversity of literary style and having been written by a great number of different authors, of whom several are unknown to us, over a period of at least a thousand years, that is, a period that in our history would stretch from the Battle of Hastings to the present day [1964]. The experts distinguish easily in the New Testament alone, for example, a Pauline style; a primitive Christology; a Johannine style; an eschatology of the Synoptics, of John, of Paul, and so forth: all of which does not always seem to coincide or even to agree. Who is to be followed? In addition to this, different notions also found in the Scriptures seem difficult to reconcile or even to harmonize: evangelical morality and life in society; present life and eschatological expectation; the Spirit and Christ glorified; the Christ of the Synoptics and the Word of St. John, and so on. But when we turn from the problems of experts to the approach of the simple in reading the Bible, a new danger awaits us: that of clinging to a few particular verses and building on them a whole conception of a religious relationship, while neglecting the balance of the whole and the rectification effected by other texts and, in fact, the synthesis. This is the usual method of procedure of the sects: the sectarian spirit is above all fundamentalist; that is, it interprets the texts materially and literally, disregarding literary styles, the hierarchy of values and the priority of reality over its verbal expression. It often takes pleasure in dwelling on the prophetic, and even apocalyptic, passages. It adopts several of these and builds everything on them by rigidly following the most violent consequences and the sequence of prohibitions or condemnations.[17]

Tradition is not disjunctive; it is synthesis and harmony. It does not skirt around the subject, isolating a few texts, but on the contrary operates from within, linking the texts to the center by situating the details in relation to the essential. It is within and by means of tradition that the Church is not Paul's or Apollos' or Cephas' without being John's, nor the Church of the struggle against the Scarlet Woman [false church], unmindful of the Mystical Body or of the Eucharist, nor the Church of the Holy Spirit as opposed to that of Christ, nor of grace without a certain legalism, nor of doctrine without prophecy, nor of prophecy without doctrine. Tradition creates a totality, a harmony, a synthesis. It lives by and teaches others to live by the comprehensive spirit of God's plan, from which unfolds and develops the whole structure of the economy: what St. Irenaeus called a *system* or *oikonomia*.[18] Clement of Alexandria, supporting a true gnosis to oppose the heretical gnosis [Gnosticism], wrote at the beginning of the third century: "Everything becomes intelligible to those who preserve the interpretation that [the Lord] has given of the Scriptures, and accept it according to the ecclesiastical rule, and this rule is the marriage bond uniting the

[17] This was already so during St. Irenaeus' time; cf. AH, 1, 8, 1.
[18] AH, 4, 33, 8 (PG 7:1077; Harvey, 2, p. 262).

law and prophets to the Testament transmitted with the coming of the Lord." [19]

The respective qualities of Scripture and tradition

Both Scripture and tradition are human and divine, but in different degrees and conditions. It would be misleading to say that Scripture was wholly divine and tradition purely human: Scripture too is human and historical; biblical studies have increasingly revealed how its composition was conditioned by literary styles, imagery and even ideas. Nevertheless, in the holy Scriptures the human element is fixed once and for all, whereas in tradition it is present throughout the whole of this tradition's historical duration. The holy Scriptures give us the word of the prophets and apostles in a human form, which, however, is the actual form given it by the prophets and apostles, while the form of the different monuments of tradition neither comes from the apostles nor is even of their period. And the form a thought takes is closely linked to the thought itself.

In both cases the divine aspect depends on the active role played by the Holy Spirit. The fact that the same Spirit operates in both is enough to ensure a certain continuity running through tradition and the Scriptures; we have seen that the Fathers, Schoolmen and Council of Trent have in fact proved the value of tradition in God's economy for revealing himself and his plan by the action of the Holy Spirit. But theology has come to distinguish with increasing clarity the action of simple *assistance* from that of true *inspiration*.[20] To think

[19] *Stromata* 6, 15, 124–25 (Staehlin, 2, pp. 494–95).

[20] If it is a question of apostolic traditions during the lifetime of the apostles, these can be equally as inspired as their writings: this is certainly the case of truths revealed by their preaching, even though they are not written down; their practical decisions may be, by their very nature, more relative and temporary. If it is

of these two as opposites, or simply to put too great a distance—amounting to a breach—between them, would be alien to the traditional line of the Fathers, the Schoolmen, Catholic ecclesiology and the Catholic Magisterium. And yet the difference is real and qualitative. It indicates two phases that correspond to what O. Cullmann calls, after St. Paul (1 Cor 3:10; Eph 2:20), the foundation, and the building, carried out through time upon these foundations laid once and for all.

Exactly the same value, therefore, should not be attributed to *tradition* and to the holy Scriptures, even if they are paid the same respect. The holy Scriptures have an absolute value that tradition has not, which is why, without being the absolute rule of every other norm, like the Protestant scriptural principle, they are the supreme guide to which any others there may be are subjected. If tradition or the Magisterium claimed to teach something contradicting the holy Scriptures, it would certainly be false, and the faithful ought to reject it.[21] Scripture is always the supreme rule and is never submitted to any other objective rule. It is, however, not the *sole* principle regulating the belief and life of the Church. To this end God has established two other principles: tradition and the Church, with her pastoral Magisterium. The Protestant Reformation has unhappily put these three realities in opposition, subjecting one

---

a question of apostolic traditions *transmitted by the Church*, the transmission itself is the object of *assistance*. If it is a question of ecclesiastical traditions formed during the historical life of the Church, they benefit at the most from assistance, and not from inspiration. "Private revelations" never form part of the faith of God's People, but assist the government by which God guides the practical life of the Church.

[21] Cf. St. Thomas Aquinas, *Com. in III Sent.*, dist. 25, q. 2, a. 1, 4 ad 3 quoted above, and *De Veritate*, q. 14, a. 10 ad 11.

to the other and setting one against the other, whereas the whole genius of tradition consisted in uniting them and recognizing their mutual relations, so closely linked that one cannot be conceived divorced entirely from the two others.[22]

Scripture and tradition do not have the same function; tradition envelops and transcends Scripture. It is more complete and could be self-sufficient (cf. above, p. 18). In fact, as Newman rightly says,[23] the Church pronounces or teaches by means of tradition, and she verifies, confirms, proves and, where necessary, criticizes tradition by means of Scripture. For Scripture is fixed; it remains as it is, without alteration. It is therefore apt by nature to be the indubitable point of reference, playing the same role in matters of doctrine as that played in the preservation of ancient monuments by what is called a witness: *testis tertius*, a third element that remains fixed and serves to measure the development of the others. In this connection, the written word has something unquestionable about it: *Scripta manent*. This is why the Church verifies and proves her teaching by Scripture. But she interprets Scripture in her tradition and decides controversies by means of her Magisterium, with reference to Scripture and tradition.

I have the impression of having dealt here with Scripture and tradition all too briefly and in a cold, dry, juridical way, using references and comparing authorities. After all, it is a question of the life of the Church, of God's People and the Body of Christ, whose Lord feeds her with his own flesh (Eph 5:29). The Fathers continually call the Scriptures the

[22] This is shown remarkably by George Tavard, *Holy Writ or Holy Church: The Crisis of the Protestant Reformation* (London: Burns and Oates, 1959).

[23] See *Via Media*, pp. 267 and 279; J. Guitton, *La philosophie de Newman* (Paris, 1933), p. 38.

Body of Christ.[24] Before being a critical reference or an argument, the sacred Text is a sort of sacrament conveying the Gospel so that we may live by it. The Fathers say that it is a means of grace and not only of information and knowledge. From another point of view, the same Fathers and the Catholic critics of the sixteenth-century Reformation came nowhere near to holding a book religion. The text as such is not the living Word of God, but only its sacrament (or sign). The decisive thing is the *act* accomplished by God and its actual operation within us. Let all sound of words cease, cease too all visual reading of printed characters on a page, and let God bring about the communion and presence, spiritual realities of which the former are but the envelope and means! The Bible is no more the reality of the religious relationship than is the Church: both of them are no more than its setting and means of transmission. All happens, finally, in the relationship between two living subjects: the Living God and the human heart.

Tradition as objectively containing things not contained in Scripture

Jesus himself wrote nothing; he did not give his apostles the mission to leave writings, but to preach. They were to preach and to transmit the message and reality of the Gospel. St. Paul considers the acts of transmitting (*paradounai*) and of receiving (*paralambanein*), or of holding and keeping (*katechein, kratein*), to be the very substance or working rule of the faith by which the communities are built up.[25]

---

[24] St. Ambrose, for example, *In Luc.*, 6, 33 (PL 15:1763); see other texts in H. de Lubac, *L'Exégèse médiévale*, 1:523.

[25] See 1 Thess 2:13; 2 Thess 2:15; 3:6; 1 Cor 11:2; 15:1–5; Gal 1:9, 12; Rom 6:17; Phil 4:9; cf. Col 2:6, 8.

It seems beyond serious question that the teaching of the apostles entrusted to the churches was a totality beside which what is formulated in their writings represents mere fragments. On the one hand, it is certain that the apostles, or their closest associates under their control and authority, founded the first churches; it was done by their preaching of the Gospel and by the institutions and practical decisions they laid down; they paid visits, they were seen to celebrate the mysteries, they were seen praying, the ardor of their souls was betrayed by the sound of their voice; their example was noted, as was their attempt to imitate their Master. On the other hand, it is certain that if the written Gospels are the direct or indirect expression of the teaching of four apostles,[26] they do not speak of absolutely everything (cf. Jn 20:30; 21:25—despite the exaggeration). But the other apostolic writings especially, namely the epistles, which are so important—and none less than the inestimably precious heritage of St. Paul—are occasional writings that are quite strictly conditioned by the particular problems of a given community. Occasional and fragmentary, St. Paul's epistles suppose that the faith is already expounded and acquired by the direct activity of the preacher. We should have no formal teaching on the Eucharist by the apostle Paul if errors and abuses had not existed in the community of Corinth. Critics would not have failed to argue from Paul's silence that the Eucharist was an invention, no doubt a late one, of the Palestinian communities, and so on. In any case, as I have already mentioned, the *written* teaching in the New Testament on the Eucharist fills a small number of verses, and the faith of the churches in this absolutely central mystery depends directly on the oral teaching of the apostles, on the example of their

---

[26] The most ancient tradition sees Mark's Gospel as the result of Peter's teaching and links Luke to St. Paul.

celebration of it and on the eucharistic reality itself, placed in the heart of the communities as an unfailing fountain of truth, much more than on the Gospel *texts*, which were written at a period when the Eucharist had been celebrated in the Church for at least thirty years. The oldest testimony we have in writing is that of St. Paul (1 Cor, in A.D. 57), the incidental nature of which has been noted. But this testimony itself is given as an echo of a *tradition* transmitted to Paul orally and passed on by him to the community at Corinth (cf. 1 Cor 11:23). When the expressions used by St. Paul in this eucharistic passage are studied carefully, they are seen to differ from St. Paul's ordinary style, and it is apparent that the content of it reached him from the Twelve. The Eucharist is an ideal example of an object of tradition.

Elsewhere, St. Paul makes allusions to decisions he has made known to the churches by oral and direct instruction, which he does not repeat in his letters.[27] He encourages his disciples to keep, and to ensure that their successors keep, what they have received from him.[28]

Theoretically, the existence of unwritten apostolic traditions appears one of the least questionable facts about the primitive Church. Doubtless Protestants would not disagree with this, in theory, but they think, or act as though they think, that such traditions are uncertain and impossible for us to verify today. The example of Papias, remarks

---

[27] Cf. 1 Thess 4:1–2, 15; 2 Thess 2:15 ("So then, brethren, stand firm and hold to the traditions which you were taught by us, either by word of mouth or by letter"); 3:6, 12; 1 Cor 11:2 ("I commend you because you ... maintain the traditions even as I have delivered them to you") and 23–25.

[28] 2 Tim 1:13–14: "Follow the pattern of the sound words which you have heard from me, in the faith and love which are in Christ Jesus; guard the truth that has been entrusted to you by the Holy Spirit who dwells within us"; 2:2: "What you have heard from me before many witnesses entrust to faithful men who will be able to teach others also."

O. Cullmann, is hardly encouraging. Papias is known to have decided, a little before the middle of the second century, to collect the living memories of those who had personally known the apostles.[29] But, as far as can be judged by the brief fragments that have been preserved for us of the *Exegeses of the Lord's Preaching*, this oral tradition conveyed a few fables. And how could we recognize an apostolic tradition today? The only sure method, conclude the Protestants, by which we can communicate with the apostles is by their writings: by these we have direct contact with them.

Perhaps there is a misunderstanding. What seems most important to me is not a few particular traditions, but what has been incorporated into the body of the Church from the apostles, over and above what they have explicitly committed to writing; this is transmitted to us as part of this same synthesis, if we enter and live in its communion, without wishing to reconstitute an ideally pure pattern according to the apostolic writings alone.

In fact, apostolic traditions do exist. As far as it is possible, not of course to draw up a list—the Council of Trent intentionally refrained from doing so—but to get some idea of them, it seems that these traditions represent above all, if not exclusively, decisions concerning rites, the liturgy, ecclesiastical discipline and practical behavior. There exists the tradition of the apostles, continued in the Church and impossible to separate from the Church's tradition, developed through the centuries by the Councils, the Fathers, the liturgy and institutions, the teaching of the Magisterium and of the Doctors, the practice of the faithful and the entire exercise of the Christian life.

[29] HE, 3, 39, 4.

A number of good Catholic authors, as I have already said, are of the opinion that it is still possible, after the Council of Trent as before it, to hold that all the truths necessary for salvation are contained, in one way or another, in the canonical Scriptures. The Magisterium itself, in its solemn pronouncements that the Immaculate Conception of Mary, Mother of God, and her corporal Assumption belong to the deposit of divine Revelation, without claiming to discover these doctrines as such in the Scriptures, declared that they were not alien to formal scriptural statements. The truth is that there is no doctrine of the Church based *solely* on Scripture independently of tradition, and none that she holds solely by oral tradition independently of Scripture: because, on the one hand, Scripture has no implications for faith independently of its meaning, given to us in the Church's delivery of it, animated by God's Spirit and, because, on the other hand, tradition possesses many links with Scripture. (1) Even if it completes the latter objectively, what it adds must, short of being a new Revelation, which is impossible, be closely connected with the written testimony; (2) in its essential dogmatic content, it gives the meaning of the Scriptures; (3) it is a synthesis, in the way already described, namely by uniting the numerous separate or partial statements to the center of Revelation, which is the economy of the Covenant in Jesus Christ of the Christian mystery. It plays this role in its interpretation of the Scriptures and also in its developments that go beyond the explicit scriptural statements. This question of development is studied in the next section of this chapter. We shall see that the spirit animating these developments, which is the condition that guarantees their homogeneity with their first formal attestation, is what is called the analogy of faith, that is, the relationship enjoyed by the various truths, linking them to each other, and all collectively to the center of Revelation.

Now, if Revelation, and the faith accompanying it, is considered as a whole and not as a multitude of separate statements, it is certainly wholly contained in the written testimony of the prophets and apostles. It is a significant historical fact that during the three centuries from the middle of the sixteenth to the middle of the nineteenth, when Catholic theology on these subjects was largely formulated under the influence of the anti-Protestant controversy, and the existence of articles of faith not contained in the Scriptures was insisted upon, this theology also treated dogma like a succession of propositions or chapters, presenting each individually and paying little attention to their organic unity. During the first half of the nineteenth century, many fine minds complained of this situation, detecting in it a profound cause of a certain stagnation in theology and of the distaste that many priests felt for it at that time. Lamennais, for example, wrote in 1829: "Theology, which is so fine in itself, so inviting and so vast, has today become, as it is taught in the majority of seminaries, no more than a petty and degenerate scholasticism, whose dryness discourages the students and gives them no idea of the totality of religion, nor of its wonderful relationship with everything that interests man and with every object of human thought. This is not the conception of St. Thomas." [30]

The Vatican Council of 1869–1870 was to echo this request for a synthesis when it indicated, in the text giving theological research its status, this way of arriving at a

---

[30] Quoted by E. Sevrin, *Dom Guéranger et La Mennais* (Paris, 1933), pp. 243–44.

religious understanding of the mysteries: by seeking for the link existing between them and with the last end of man.[31]

On the contrary, also during the nineteenth century, it was the same men who profoundly renewed the concept of tradition who rejoined the main current of thought of the Fathers and advocated a theology organically united around its center, "the great work that reconciles man with God, the principles dealing with the relationship of the believer with Jesus Christ": this phrase is by Möhler,[32] one of the thinkers who worked the hardest, at the same time for the idea of tradition and toward the idea of a doctrinal synthesis centered on the Christian mystery. Our own time, fed from the deep sources of Scripture, the Fathers and the liturgy, and having rediscovered the role of the "kerygma" in the apostolic and teaching task of the Church, is once more firmly convinced of the immense importance of a theology built as a synthesis around the Christian mystery. Once more it is willing to admit that in this sense everything is found in Scripture. But it is evident that this view is held flexibly, in a sense that is not equivalent to the Protestant *sola Scriptura*, and in such a way that it does not contradict the theory according to which there exist in the Church's doctrine separate truths, not contained as such in the holy Scriptures.

Among these truths the first would be the canon, that is, the official, binding list of the writings held by the Church to be inspired, in the dogmatic sense of the word.

The importance of the question of a canon of Scriptures is not always grasped, owing to ignorance of the existence of a great number of writings that claim to be by prophets,

[31] Sess. 3, c. 4 (Denz., 1796).
[32] *Symbolik*, a. 37.

apostles or others connected with the history of the Gospels. There are about fifty accounts claiming to be Gospels or of apostolic origin. The Church recognizes only four Gospels as canonical and calls the others "apocryphal". There exist an almost equal number of Jewish apocryphal writings; the studies about the Essenes of the shores of the Dead Sea and the manuscripts of Qumran have, for the last fifteen years [1949–1964], directed attention to them again and added to our knowledge of them.

What then determines the fact that we can accept certain writings and not others as the norm of the faith by which God's People must live? Scripture itself contains neither list nor indication. To say, with Karl Barth, that Scripture presents itself as canonical, since it speaks to us of Jesus Christ, is an unsatisfactory answer: the apocryphal gospels of Christ's childhood also speak to us of him; they speak of him differently from the canonical Gospels, and it may be claimed that the Jesus Christ they show us is not the one we know by faith, but here the faith of the Church is appealed to as criterion. The content of the writings will serve as a guide only when placed in a certain interpretation—that of the illumination of the faith transmitted by the Church.

Here a distinction must be made between the canon as a closed list of writings and the principle of a canon, that is, of a collection of writings forming a norm. A list was not compiled at the first attempt. It was finally promulgated in the Church only in the "Decree for the Jacobites" (February 4, 1441) and at the Council of Trent, which also drew up a formal list of the seven sacraments. The two cases are similar. In both it is a question of a Church dogma whose link with scriptural Revelation is analogous. The basic principle of a canon is apostolic: it was already Jewish, and

Christianity merely extended its application to the apostolic writings. In this respect, it consists of the idea that everything done, decided and written by the apostles or by certain of their companions approved by them, in founding and building up the churches, possessed a normative value. The real problem, for the Church, was to recognize what was apostolic. She did this by using two criteria jointly: one historical, consisting in collecting the testimonies on the composition of a certain text by an apostle or someone in his name; the other dogmatic, consisting in judging a writing according to its tenor, in the light of the Church's faith, governed by the tradition she had received from the apostles and by which she lived. The principle of the canon thus had its origin in Revelation, to which the Scriptures are the witness or monument. Its application has been developed and has sought to express itself; the fluctuations of the canon have followed only the fluctuations of the attribution of an apostolic origin to a given writing. Finally, as for any dogma in the narrow sense of the word, the Magisterium intervened to fix tradition, which is a good example of the role that it was seen to possess in the last chapter. In this way, all the governing principles of the faith cooperate in the constitution of the canon: the Revelation made to the prophets and apostles (of which Scripture is the memorial), tradition, the Church and her Magisterium.

It is not that the Church and her Magisterium actually create the canon; even less do they endow Scripture with its authority, as mistakenly rather than intentionally certain Catholic apologists have sometimes maintained. With this dogma, as with the others, Church and Magisterium simply recognize the truth established by *God's* action, submit to it and, since they are responsible for it, proclaim it with authority, making it into a Church law.

A German dogmatic theologian of the middle of the nineteenth century, J. E. von Kuhn, summarized the position of the Fathers on the question of the relationship between Scripture and tradition in the four following propositions: (1) Scripture contains everything; but (2) it can be read correctly only in and with tradition; (3) this latter consists in understanding the Scriptures; (4) in addition there exist traditions. Taken separately, these statements are an insufficient expression of the living synthesis realized by the three means instituted by God—Scripture, tradition and the Church herself and her Magisterium—for the sustenance and regulation of the faith of the Church. There is cooperation between them, and not competition, under the action of the Holy Spirit, who is their underlying, common principle of operation. The insistence upon the role of tradition and the instituted ministry is one of the many ways in which the Church lives the belief and Christianity of the apostles, safeguarding both the purity and entirety of the religious relationship, as God established it in Jesus Christ. Among these ways, holy Scripture has the position and privilege of being the supreme objective rule, but it must not be imagined that this role brings it into opposition with the Church or divides it from her, because this is not how God established his Covenant. Among the differences that remain between the Reformers and ourselves, the most decisive and radical does not arise from the conception of Scripture but of the Church. The Protestants want a Church ceaselessly renewing herself by a dramatic and precarious confrontation with the Word of God. Together with the Fathers, we see the Church as the continuous communication, through space and time, of the mystical community born from the Lord's institution and Pentecost.

TRADITION AS A DEVELOPMENT THROUGH HISTORY

Tradition is not merely the mechanical transmission of a passive deposit. The very concept implies the delivery of an object from the possession of one person to another, and therefore the transition from one living being to another. It is *incorporated* into a *subject*, a *living* subject.

A living subject necessarily puts something of himself into what he receives. When he receives a teaching, whether it is by word of mouth, by example or even from a written book, it always assumes a certain quality of dialogue. Words, even when written, of their very nature include something that arouses a response in the person addressed. A message, and this is particularly true of the apostolic message, is destined for someone *so that* he may live by it.

The New Testament presents Mary as the perfect example of the believer. She accepts the Word gladly, and this is how she becomes the Mother of God. She keeps the Word in her heart (Lk 2:19, 51). In these simple words there is an extraordinary depth of meaning, and one that is specifically biblical. "Word" and "heart" in the Bible are full of meaning; the same is true of "to keep", whichever Greek verb is used in the different passages. It is something quite different from merely memorizing a fact: it describes an action of living fidelity, the living fidelity of the mind that ponders the meaning of what it has heard, drawing consequences and seeking to define precisely what is true and what is false. The Church, in Fr. Hugo Rahner's magnificent phrase, is "the Mary of the history of the world". She imitates and prolongs this meditation through the centuries and will not cease until history has said its final word, given all it has to give, and asked its final question.

But even with this mental activity, it is not a matter of a purely intellectual fidelity of reasoning. It is one of the most solid tenets of Christian experience, and one of those that Christian apologists have not ceased to maintain ever since the post-apostolic period, that there is no rectitude possible in the domain of faith and salvation, even as regards its knowledge, without a certain rectitude of life. Theophilus of Antioch, martyred in approximately A.D. 180, gave Autolycus, his pagan interrogator, who asked him condescendingly, "Show me your God", the following brave and wise reply: "Show me your man and I will show you my God; show me what kind of man you are . . . ; if you are a certain type of man, if your 'heart' (that is, your inner disposition) is sound, then you will be able to see God, and I will show him to you." St. Gregory the Great wrote in his turn, five centuries later: "To fail to *listen* to the Word is to fail to put it into practice in one's life." In the New Testament, "to keep the Word" is the same as to build on the foundation that is Christ, to take root and grow in Christ.[33] This even supposes from us something more than a wholly passive receptivity: it supposes an exchange of gifts. Certainly God gives everything, and yet we must feed his action within us with our own living being. We must feed our life with the Word, but this is impossible without giving ourselves, without feeding the Word with our lives. It is a mutual gift, an exchange, a sort of banquet in which Christ who is truth, on the one hand, and man, so long as he remains faithful, on the other, are mutually guest and nourishment: they are incorporated one within the other and really form a "covenant".

[33] Theophilus of Antioch, *To Autolycus*; St. Gregory, *Hom. 18 in Evangel.*, 1 (PL 76:1150).

It is not enough to say that there is a living subject; it must be added that this subject lives *in history* and that historicity is one of its inherent features, without, however, implying that its truth is relative or that it is nothing more than the successive and changing thought of men. Tradition implies and even tolerates no alteration in its objective content. It is a communication from one living person to another, but it is the communication of a definite object that retains the identity of its inner nature. This communication is made, however, in a history to which it does not remain alien. In other words, this history does not act simply as a setting for it, like a backdrop on a film set, which changes behind the actors without affecting them. It affects the conservation, transmission and even the content of what is kept and passed on in a certain way that does not destroy its identity. Tradition is certainly a continuity through time that flows past, but it is a *historical* continuity: it is the permanence of the past in the present, from the heart of which it prepares the future. "Tradition", wrote M. Blondel in his articles of 1904, "anticipates the future and prepares to shed light upon it by its very effort to remain faithful to the past." [34] But the fidelity here described is not a simple conservation and mechanical reproduction of the past; it is the fidelity of a living being who lives in history, one who *has a life history*.

This history is a reply to the questions of time, for it is first the history of men and of the world. It is not a peaceful reverie; it is full of inventions, of questions and initiative. It

[34] Compare this to what the Orthodox thinker Paul Evdokimov says: "In a very paradoxical way, thanks to the Witness who subsists, Tradition, though part of the past, is in harmony with the future. 'The Spirit has spoken through the prophets' and it is from the Church's prophetical dimension that he draws *in the past*, in Christ, what he foretells *for the future*" (*L'Orthodoxie* [Neuchâtel and Paris, 1959], p. 196).

is the setting in which the evolution of the world is enacted, not only by the slow, inexorable progress of cosmic nature, but through human activity: the conflicts, advances and set-backs of men. All this demands answers from the Gospel, whose deposit is carried by the Church as by a holy ark upon a turbulent sea; and the Gospel has its own point of view to present on all these matters. If God, having said all that he had to tell us in Jesus Christ, no longer inter-venes in the world by a new public Revelation, he expects to see his People giving forth the Word it has received, once again—a thousand times again—for the healing of the nations (cf. Rev 22:2). The Gospel must be preached to every creature (Mk 16:15), but the creature is not waiting for it, expectant and inactive; it is advancing through time down every path and in every direction imaginable.

In the Church herself errors come from active but indoc-ile minds. When Arius formulated his conception of the Word as a sort of divine demiurge a little below God himself, it was not enough to repeat St. John's verses "The Father and I are one" and "The Word was God", since these texts did not stop him. It was necessary to become familiar with the content of the apostolic testimony, still inexplicit on that ques-tion, and to formulate this content in a way that, though new with regard to the literal scriptural text, would answer satisfactorily the question troubling the Catholic con-science. When the Jansenists proposed a conception of the Christian life and of the relationship between nature and grace based on quotations from St. Augustine, it was not enough to repeat the statements of St. Paul, the Councils, the Fathers and St. Thomas, since these texts did not change the over-rigid Jansenist idea of authentic Christianity. The Church had to say something new that, without breaking the continuity of its doctrinal identity, would define its belief and eliminate the error satisfactorily. The truth of the religious relationship in its most delicate and decisive aspect was also at issue. And there have been similar cases down the ages. What is more, I have quoted only replies to errors. There is the immense field of replies needed to simple questions and requests, silent or voiced, explicit or unconscious, that men address to the Church, bearer of the Gospel message, in each vicissitude of the drama or comedy that constitutes their history. The good scholar in the Kingdom of Heaven should bring forth from his treasure-house new things as well as old.

There is also the new expression the "new editions" and rediscoveries of the unique message. In any case, there is no lack of occupations to fill the time. Even if there were no errors and urgent questions—which is impossible to imagine!—the time would still be employed by the actual living of their Christian life by the faithful of Jesus Christ, seeking God, loving him with their whole hearts and embracing their human brethren in the same love. There would and always will be in the Church a contemplation of the mysteries, a meditation of the holy Scriptures and an experience of God's presence and intimate activity. Nietzsche has spoken of "new editions" of philosophy. Throughout the centuries, either as a result of reflection alone or because the world picture and vision of reality have changed, age-old wisdom and philosophical ideas are rediscovered. A new thinker or school of thought then "reedits" Plato, Augustine or Hegel. The old sap, still living, brings life to a new tree. It is not simply a repetition of the old, like a new impression of an old record; it is an original expression, clothed in a new vocabulary; the old, belonging to eternity, is indeed repeated, but not in its former state;

deployed to reply to new problems, it uses new resources drawn from a given period, fashioned by human activity. The problems of the fifth century and the resources of Augustine are not those of the third century and Hippolytus; the problems of the thirteenth century and the resources of Thomas Aquinas are not those of the fifth century and Augustine. Today we find ourselves equipped with resources that are new again and faced with problems and possibilities as yet unknown. "In order to remain faithful to herself and her mission, the Church must continually make an effort at creative invention. Paul had to be inventive in order to cope with the problem of the Gentiles who were obliged to enter into a Church that was heir to the Synagogue. The same applies to the Greek Fathers in the face of Hellenistic culture, and also to Saint Thomas in the face of Arabic philosophy and knowledge. We, indeed, for our part, must do the same in the face of the problems of our day." [35]

Tradition, then, comprises two equally vital aspects: one of development and one of conservation. This is why some see tradition eminently as a safeguard for the purity of the deposit, at the risk of cutting the present off from the future, while others see it eminently as a way of opening the present to the future, in the search for a total synthesis. There is a sort of tension or dialectic between purity and totality, neither of which should be sacrificed. It is understandable that the Magisterium, whose chief mission is to keep and transmit a deposit, should be more concerned with the purity and that this should be its duty. Faced with time's challenges,

[35] Hans Urs von Balthasar, *Presence and Thought: Essay on the Religious Philosophy of Gregory of Nyssa*, trans. Mark Sebanc (San Francisco: Ignatius Press, 1995), p. 12. Concerning the entire question of development, briefly mentioned in the following pages, see *Do Dogmas Change?* by H. Rondet, S.J. (New York: Hawthorn Books, 1961).

the Church's first reaction is always an instinct of conservation. This is natural. But it is also part of her mission to
display the Gospel as extensively as possible to mankind, which
is growing ceaselessly, not only externally and numerically,
but also internally.

This conservative reflex is also shared at times by the
most careful and best-informed men in history. Dedicated
to the study of documents, they are apt to refuse to recognize the existence of definite ideas, albeit subconscious and
unexpressed, beyond the explicit statement of a document.
Since the advent of the historical and documentary sciences, that is, since the sixteenth century, there have been
periodic protests against innovation, protests made in the
name of textual authority, and against "living tradition", in
the name of the monuments of tradition. It is no coinci-
dence that the expression "living tradition" was first used
during the Jansenist debate. The Jansenists were followers
of the sacred Text, men of the past and of the literal words
of St. Augustine, who, according to them, condemned the
practice of their time. Their conception of tradition was
documentary, historical and static.[36] On this matter, the Gallicans willingly joined forces with them and indeed often
possessed a remarkable knowledge of ecclesiastical history.
Using this knowledge they contested certain developments
of papal power. Such remained the position of Döllinger
and a certain number of professors and canonists with regard
to the dogmas defined by the Council of 1869–1870 concerning the universal jurisdiction and infallibility of the
Supreme Pontiff. The Old Catholic schism was a result of
this. They all appealed to the "Canon of St. Vincent of
Lérins", that is, the rule formulated by him in 434 giving

---

[36] See EH, p. 239 f.

the antiquity and universality of a belief manifested in the unanimity of its profession as criterion of dogmatic truth: *Quod ubique, quod semper, quod ab omnibus,* "what has been believed everywhere, always and by everyone".[37] St. Vincent's intention was certainly a conservative one; he was fighting the "novelties" of Augustinism, in the domain of theology and grace, and it is this same intention that underlies the famous text where the monk from Lérins states the need for development, and whose final phrase, quoted by the First Vatican Council, has almost become the charter of this theory:

> But, it will be said, is not religion then open to any progress in the Church of Christ? On the contrary there must be progress, considerable progress. Who would be sufficiently hostile to mankind and to God to oppose it? But a reservation must be made; this progress must constitute a real progress for the faith, and not an alteration: the characteristic of progress being that each element grows and yet remains itself, while the characteristic of alteration is that one thing is transformed into another. Therefore, let intelligence, knowledge and wisdom increase and progress greatly, those of individuals as well as those of the community, those of a single man

[37] Theologians show that this "canon" cannot be used negatively, that is, to *exclude* all true development by accepting only what is found always and everywhere in the past. In addition, this "canon" makes no mention of the established or assisted Magisterium. It is valid, however, in its positive sense: what is found to be held definitely always and everywhere, what has always been believed by everyone, belongs definitely to tradition. What is more, this "canon" is a good expression, against certain exaggerations of the Magisterium or of the "mind of the Church", of the need to refer them to the certified content of tradition handed down, of the immense value of antiquity and lastly of the importance of agreement as the sign of truth and the action of the Holy Spirit. It would be profitable to read Newman's assessment of the canon of St. Vincent of Lérins, so often quoted by Anglicans, in his *Essay on the Development of Doctrine*; see also St. Vincent of Lérins, *Commonitorium.*

as well as those of the whole Church, according to the ages
and centuries—but on condition that it be greatly in keeping with their particular nature, that is to say in the same
dogma, the same sense and the same thought.[38]

Progress "in the same sense and the same thought" may
simply be the unfolding of an idea that is already present. It
may also be the development of the latent qualities of an
accepted idea or reality believed. It may be said that the
dogma of Nicaea (the Son being "consubstantial" with the
Father) simply clarifies the content of an idea already contained explicitly in the Bible; the same is true for the dogma
of Christ's real presence in the Eucharist, for which the
term "transubstantiation" has been declared highly fitting.
But the dogma of the Immaculate Conception or that of
the corporal Assumption of Mary, Mother of God, can
scarcely pass as the simple explanation of a formal statement of Revelation, certified scripturally. And yet these dogmas have strong ties with Revelation, in the setting and by
means of what is called "the analogy of faith".

This expression, borrowed from St. Paul (Rom 12:6),
signifies, in theology, the relationship and proportions existing between the different statements or articles that have
been revealed: relationship and proportions such that new
statements, not made explicitly in the documents of Revelation, appear possible and even necessary; a little in the
same way that Leverrier was able, merely by means of cal-
culation and without experimental or factual evidence, to
state the existence of the planet Saturn, which was subsequently confirmed by telescope. Things are such, their

[38] St. Vincent of Lérins, *Commonitorium*, c. 23. Vatican Council I, sess. 3, c.
4 (Denz., 1800).

balance and the relationship between them are such, that a new idea is produced as certain, and even at times as necessary.

We have also seen, in a preceding chapter, Maurice Blondel's criticism of what he called "historicism", which is closely related to a purely historical and documentary conception of tradition. The Church, said Blondel, possesses other sources of knowledge besides the mere documents. She has the experience of Christian reality as such continually present within her, motivated and directed by the Holy Spirit. Tradition, added Blondel, is precisely the place where the synthesis is realized between the historical transmission and the present experience, which, thus united, produce, in the present and in preparation for the future, a profound knowledge of Christian reality transcending the text of the document with which it started. Tradition is not merely memory; it is actual presence and experience. It is not purely conservative, but, in a certain way, creative. After almost twenty centuries of existence, it presents a certain additional value with regard to its primary statements, at least insofar as we can deduce these from the documents. From this aspect of development, the tradition of the more or less distant past has prepared the tradition of today, and today's tradition will prepare that of the more or less distant future. In its actual role as channel, since it is not inert but living, it is to a certain extent a source. By nourishing the tissues of the body, the blood is rejuvenated in the arteries that carry it. Tradition is the living artery that receives an increase of the very life it communicates, in its act of transmission.

It is true that what flows afresh in the transmitting channel comes entirely from *the* original and unique source, which we know to be Jesus Christ and his saving Gospel. This is an absolute and unequivocal fact. But this source is not restricted to the content of a text; it is an ever-active reality, alive in

the Church. The deposit in its primitive documentary form
is not the sole principle responsible for the value of what is
communicated two, ten or twenty centuries later. A life force,
wholly governed by the deposit and produced in living, spiritual beings by the Spirit of Life himself, transforms the channel into a sort of source with regard to what it transmits.
The value of what is delivered after a living transmission comes
mainly from what is itself transmitted, but *also* from the incor-
poration within itself, in its transmission, of the fruit of the
Holy Spirit's action allowing it to share the life of the very
deposit it carries.

Tradition, therefore, in its historical journey, is as much
development as it is memory and conservation. In this way it
earns interest, as it were, during the centuries, which is added
to its capital foundation. Although I live in a moment of
time subsequent to it, what I receive is still the apostolic
heritage: "the faith which was once for all delivered to the
saints" (Jude 3), but as it has been lived in and by the Church,
in the communion of saints. It is given to us, but also asked
of us, "to comprehend with all the saints what is the breadth
and length and height and depth, and to know the love of
Christ which surpasses knowledge, that [we] may be filled
with all the fulness of God" (Eph 3:18–19). I am called to
live today in a religious relationship, in the form given it by
Jesus Christ once and for all, but also in the way it is presented, and in *certain* respects enriched, for having been lived,
pondered and expressed by generations of believers inhab-
ited and vivified by the Spirit of Pentecost.

If I consider more particularly the treasure of knowledge
contained in this heritage at a given moment, I can attempt
to make a synthesis of all that is valid at least of the developments acquired through the centuries. It has been noted
above that one of the tasks of the Magisterium is to test and

appreciate what is expressed in the Church; it is under its guidance that I shall discern the valid from the invalid. Simple believers make this synthesis without realizing it, simply by living their Christianity within the fellowship of the Church, as it is presented to them today, taught by the living pastoral Magisterium and also by the leading thinkers in the Church. The theologians and thinkers, without being exempt, since they are first and foremost believers, attempt to make this synthesis on their own account, though remaining under the guidance of established pastors (see Acts 20:28), by the laborious means of scientific investigation. This is their guiding principle as theologians, for theology is the form or scientific culture of the faith, the form it takes in a human mind using its reasoning powers to understand it more fully.[39] "Positive theology" is the name for that part of the science of theology that takes, as the foundation of its contemplation of the mysteries, the richest possible "material" of tradition, thus attempting to include in its knowledge all that has already been said by the geniuses and saints who have lived and meditated on their faith before us.

The reader, who is possibly not familiar with the sacred sciences, will thus understand something that may have astonished or troubled him, if he has encountered it. Accustomed to the human sciences, which are based on the immediate experience of reality, he may have found it strange that clergy so often appeal to authorities and quote texts and references. In the 1960s G. Mounin, a Communist, spoke of his confusion when faced with a Catholic treatise concerned with water: all kinds of authors were quoted who had spoken of water in a religious context, without a single reference being

---

[39] See M. D. Chenu, O.P., *Is Theology a Science?* (New York: Hawthorn Books, 1959).

made to the direct experience of the liquid in question or of
its physical properties. This example is rather amusing, but,
in fact, it results from the particular structure of theology, a
science of religious realities deriving from what is revealed
to us by *texts*: in the first place, naturally, and principally, that
of the holy Scriptures, and, in the second place, those that
reveal the Church's historical tradition. These texts are not
of equal value, or at least of equal authority. The main ones,
in a descending order of importance, are the decisions of the
Councils and popes, the liturgy, the Church Fathers, the Doctors and theologians and the monuments, of which the principal ones will be studied in the next chapter. In theological
treatises the arguments advanced in turn are often preceded
by two or three paragraphs, attempting to support them by
means of authoritative witnesses. The first paragraph is introduced by the words *Probatur ex Scriptura*, "Proved by Scripture", and consists in quoting a certain number of verses from
the Old and New Testaments. The second paragraph is introduced by the words *Probatur ex Traditione*, "Proved by Tradition", and it collects a number of testimonies taken from the
monuments of tradition listed above. Often a third paragraph invokes decisions by the Magisterium.

This system of theological proof evidently assumes the existence of a certain continuity, and even homogeneity, between
Scripture, the Church and tradition, in spite of the different
quality of these three realities. As has been already stated, the
whole Catholic position implies an inner, mutual relationship, a link, an interaction and almost a mutual presence,
between these three realities, which the Reformation unfortunately separated and placed in opposition to each other.
Faced with new predicaments and in reply to contemporary
problems, the Councils and the Magisterium, the Fathers
and Doctors continue to manifest the mystery of God and

of the true religious relationship established by the prophets, the Lord and his apostles. For Revelation, according to the Fathers, the Councils, medieval theologians and Catholic teaching, includes, in its diffusion through human history (which, through the operation of the Spirit of God, is a continuation of the history of salvation), the totality of God's manifestation, as the Church understands the implications of the true religious relationship more and more fully, under the influence of the Holy Spirit.

"Tradition", then, assumes a second meaning or secondary quality. It was first the pure and simple transmission of the sacred deposit. It is also the explanation of this deposit, elaborated through its being lived, defended and explained generation after generation by the People of God. Scripture, the prophetic and apostolic witness to God's plan, is *explained* by tradition; in this respect there is *more* in the Church's word (and in some eventual "definition" of the extraordinary Magisterium) than in the text of Scripture studied philologically and understood historically. But the Magisterium and the Church must continually return to the point of origin, the norm of the transmitted deposit. In doing this they are reimmersed in a plenitude greater than themselves: there is *more* in the original source than in the stream it feeds: "Therefore every scribe who has been trained for the kingdom of heaven is like a householder who brings out of his treasure what is new and what is old" (Mt 13:52).

I am aware that Protestants would be very loath to accept the views that I have just expounded. I think that at the deepest level this is due to their determination to make the religious relationship depend on nothing other than God (on his Word), so that he alone effects our salvation. It is equally due to their lack of a satisfactory ecclesiology and, it seems to me, to the fact that the Protestant starts from the Word of

God as the principle from which his religion reaches him, and in practical terms from the sacred *Text*, considered as being the Word of God, while the Catholic starts from the reality of Christianity itself that reaches him in and by the Church, ever since the apostles. The Protestant rejects what he does not find formally in the Scriptures. The Catholic is unable to justify his position entirely by referring to a text; but, regarding it as an element of the Christian reality he has received, he can *rediscover* a certain testimony in Scripture. Thus the Christian reality (tradition) needs the verification of documents, without being rigorously and restrictively bound to the letter of the text as such. It must justify itself by the text, but from the standpoint of its present belief it *recognizes in the text* certain proofs not revealed by a simple reading of the text. The text controls it, but tradition clarifies the text, which is no more than a witness of facts and realities by which the Church lives and that she possesses. The *deposit* is richer than its written expression.

It is worth noting, but should not surprise those who have followed me thus far, that the realities held by the Catholic and rejected by the Protestant as not proven by Scripture— such inner realities as those founded on a sense of God's presence, activity and exactingness in the creature he sanctifies: the Marian mystery, the religious life (monachism), the dignity of consecrated virginity, the eucharistic presence—are realities that concern the religious relationship in its inmost truth; they are in no way secondary, but intimate and almost secret. Their biblical foundations are very solid but are revealed only in tradition.

At the end of this third chapter we can obtain a fairly precise idea of the different aspects covered by the word "tradition". If asked to clarify these schematically I should suggest the following:

Traditions are decisions that become norms under certain conditions, still to be defined, and that are not formally contained in the Scriptures. They can come from Jesus, from the apostles or from the Church, being respectively divine, apostolic or ecclesiastical. They can be permanent or transitory. It may be deduced that, without detriment to their dogmatic implications, they concern worship and discipline directly.

Tradition has three, or even four, aspects or meanings:

1. It is the transmission of the whole Gospel, that is, of the Christian mystery, whatever form it takes: Scripture, preaching, profession of faith, sacraments and external forms of worship, customs and rules. And this is so in a twofold sense: first, objectively in the content of the deposit, and second, in the act of its transmission.

2. In the content thus transmitted, concerning the truth of the Christian mystery or the Covenant, it is possible to distinguish between the objects (the Scriptures, above all, and sacraments and institutions) and their interpretation or meaning. Tradition is therefore the interpretation or meaning given to the realities transmitted in the community to which they were entrusted, which lives by them and hands them on. With regard to Scripture, tradition is a certain way of using and interpreting it: it is read within the context of the Christian mystery, according to an interpretation that is equally centered on Christ, the Church and eschatology, and makes use of the analogy of faith. This objective sense is frequently found in the writings of the early Fathers; it coincides largely, but not completely, with the rule of faith, in the objective sense of the word, which is also that given it by the Fathers.

3. This interpretation is elaborated and expressed in a succession of static testimonies forming a system, either in writings or in other monuments: institutions, liturgy, art, customs,

and so forth. These expressions taken collectively are often called "tradition"—as in the *Probatur ex Traditione* of our manuals, where "tradition" in fact signifies the monuments of tradition.

This interpretation exists in the very genius of the Christian community (*ecclesia*), in germinal form diffused throughout the community, like the mental climate or personal culture of a people, or the particular *ethos* of a family. Tradition signifies, then, the Catholic spirit together with the living manner in which the whole apostolic deposit, whose subject is the Church, is transmitted.

CHAPTER IV

THE MONUMENTS OR WITNESSES
OF TRADITION

It is the last meaning of the word "tradition" whose content must now be defined. What are these monuments or witnesses of tradition that enable us to reach it? Do they express it so adequately that they may simply be said to *be* tradition? In this case tradition would be limited, not only to what has been received from the past, but to that part of the heritage that is contained in documents. The Magisterium would belong to the experts of biblical and Christian history. Is this acceptable? Once we have listed the principal witnesses of tradition we shall have to examine the relationship existing between tradition and its monuments.

THE MONUMENTS

The Word of God, which is the major source of the salvation offered to us on the basis of faith, does not reach each man individually and directly. It reaches us by mediation and in stages. These intermediaries of the Word are obviously not all of equal importance. First of all comes holy Scripture, which is the measure and norm of all the others, since it *is* the Word *of God*. By means of inspiration God is responsible for its human form, which makes an intermediary of it. St. Cyprian called him *divinae traditionis caput et origo*, "the principle and origin of divine tradition".[1] Cyprian limits the use of the words *traditio, tradere* to the *first* delivery by God or by Christ; he does not apply them to ecclesiastical tradition, with the result that his expression has a special meaning peculiar to him, but which is striking, nonetheless. It would be interesting to speak of Scripture, but it falls outside the present subject. It is indeed possible to take tradition in its extensive or comprehensive sense, as the transmission of all that God has given us to live by, in which case Scripture is the principal element. But tradition is generally considered as something other than Scripture, which is how we have considered it, and it is there that we meet the real problems. This is why I shall simply indicate the place of Scripture without mentioning it further among the witnesses of tradition.

The texts of the Magisterium are next in importance immediately after the holy Scriptures, at least with regard to its major pronouncements: the dogmas, in the true sense of the word, the solemn teaching, either of the extraordinary Magisterium—by the Councils or the Pope—or of the ordinary and universal Magisterium of the bishops at the head of the different churches. Apart from these major pronouncements, the Magisterium of the bishops, popes and Councils has taught in many ways, over a range containing tones and semitones and the finest shades of nuance. The totality of documents by the Magisterium is so massive that no collection has ever attempted to encompass it entirely. There exist excellent collections of Ecumenical or local Councils, but these stop at the beginning of the most recent

[1] *Epist.* 74, 10.

period with regard to the local Councils.[2] There exist collections of papal bulls (the Turin edition, 1867–1872, comprises twenty-five volumes), but they are sadly incomplete and without critical value. For the present period the *Acta Sanctae Sedis* (1865–1908), which became the *Acta Apostolicae Sedis* in 1909, publish the official acts of the Pope and of the Roman Congregations. But it is impossible to find a collection of episcopal decisions and diocesan catechisms, and yet they are the documents of the ordinary Magisterium. And what about preaching, which is the basic act of teaching in the Church?

A famous collection exists that is useful and handy; it is an *Enchiridion* of creeds, definitions and pronouncements concerning faith and morals, produced by Henry Denzinger (1854) and Fr. Cl. Bannwart (from 1908). It is indispensable for clerics in their teaching and research. The layman's notion of the mysterious "Denzinger", if he has heard of it, is vague. He pictures a very learned collection of volumes, accessible only to the erudite. In fact it is a sort of theological almanac, giving extracts of the most striking passages of the principal documents of the Magisterium of a decisive nature. The collection is obviously incomplete, containing no texts of local Councils and absolutely none of the bishops' ordinary Magisterium.

It is remarkably useful but has the great drawback of baldly presenting documents in isolation from the historical and

---

[2] The most complete collections that may be found in libraries are those of Labbe and Cossart, 17 vols. (1671–1672), Harduin (1715 et seq.) and Mansi, 53 vols. (Florence, 1759, reedited and completed by Msgr. L. Petit). The decrees of the ecumenical Councils have recently been collected in one volume: *Conciliorum oecumenicorum decreta*, ed. G. Alberigo, P. Joannou, C. Leonardi and P. Brodi (Rome: Herder, 1962). [Yves Congar compiled this list in 1963.—ED.]

theological culture that alone enables them to be correctly interpreted. Of course, this could scarcely be avoided, but we must not become victims or dupes of a practical necessity, as would be the case if we read these texts while remaining oblivious of the historical and philological context, in which context alone they can be understood fairly and accurately, or if, in a different way, we merely sought canonical decisions in these monuments of tradition, without going beyond the juridical aspect in order to reach the religious and theological life force of these witnesses and to enter into communion with the faith of the Church and of preceding generations. By its very nature Denzinger encourages this unfortunate reduction of dogma into legal propositions, each possessing a coefficient of authority and juridical obligation—"of faith", "near to the faith",[3] "certain", etc.

A juridical approach to the documents concentrates on the act of the authority that produced the texts and the degree of the resulting obligation; it leads to a neglect of the value of thought and treasure of contemplation concealed in the text itself. In the language of the Scholastics it might be said to be concerned with the *quo* (by which authority? with what obligation?) and not with the *quod* (what content?). There is also the risk of dissecting theology in this way, by reducing it to a succession of isolated statements, each having its "proof" from authority, and of losing sight of the profound unity, the mutual relationship and the organic structure of all the parts. Finally, there is the risk of ignoring the construction and scale of values that exist in the vast domain of Catholic teaching and, failing to consider the *content*, of putting on the same level all

---

[3] *Proximum fidei*: a truth is so called because it appears to follow from infallible decisions of the Church without being expressly formulated.—TRANS.

that is pronounced by the same authority. This remark applies equally to holy Scripture. From the point of view of authority and guarantee, all that it contains is equally certain, but from the point of view of content all has not the same value, for Scripture possesses a center of interest and intention, with regard to which all that is stated in it has a greater or lesser importance according to its relation with the center. And because of this the totality finds its unity, like the leaves and twigs on a living tree, by the intermediary of the main branches, as opposed to what they would be if cut up and distributed in piles of equal weight.

This is not to deny the existence of distinctions in a juridical approach to the documents of the Magisterium and of tradition; on the contrary, there are many. Indeed, from the sixteenth century onward, a special treatise was drawn up, which had been attempted several times before, but in a very rudimentary form. This treatise bears the somewhat disconcerting title *Loci theologici*.[4] By this was meant a distribution into different categories the material that theologians can develop, each with its own degree of weight or authority: decrees of the Councils, the popes, the Fathers, the liturgy, theologians and so on. It is sometimes called *theological criteriology*. These treatises decide which conditions are necessary for the documents of such and such a category to possess a certain authority. What weight, what amount of authority, should be given to the agreement of the bishops, to that of the Church Fathers, to each taken individually or as a body, or to the liturgy—to the existence,

[4] The expression "places" was borrowed from the art of rhetoric, where it signified the *bases* of arguments that could be skillfully advanced in a speech. It has a completely different sense in Protestant theology, in which the "theological places" are the different chapters or treatises of theology, for example, the place of predestination or the place of the sacrament of baptism.

for example, of a liturgical feast commemorating a certain event[5]—to the agreement of the theologians?

These particulars are useful and even necessary; what is more, they speak in their own defense. But the reader anxious to acquire a religious culture does not expect to find repeated here what he can find elsewhere. It is my aim, rather, and I hope it fulfills his expectations, to give the inner characteristics of the principal witnesses of tradition, with the exception of the holy Scriptures and the texts of the Magisterium, in which it is best possible to reach the very soul of tradition, considered above all, as it has been, as the living transmission of the spirit of Christianity. These witnesses are the liturgy, the Fathers and the practice and spontaneous gestures by which the faith is expressed.

The liturgy

In his *Institutions liturgiques* Dom Guéranger wrote: "It is in the liturgy that the Spirit who inspired the Scriptures speaks again; the liturgy is tradition itself at its highest degree of power and solemnity." No finer expression of the truth could be found. It is this that will be examined from the three most decisive aspects presented by tradition: as a means other than writing of transmitting everything in a way that is profoundly educative; as a means, in some cases, of transmitting something not contained formally in Scripture; and as an interpretation of the holy Scriptures that really brings home their meaning.

[5] Example: Is the existence of a feast of the Presentation of the Blessed Virgin Mary in the Temple equivalent to an authentic affirmation of the event's historical truth? The answer is no.

*a. The liturgy as a means other than writing of transmitting every-
thing, in a way that is profoundly educative*

The liturgy is not exclusively a form of instruction, even
though it is wholly instructive and includes some formal periods of instruction. It is an active memorial, a presence and a
realization, in short, a celebration of the Christian mystery
itself—of the whole Christian mystery, for if the liturgy celebrates particular mysteries successively, according to its
well-known sequence of feasts—Christmas, Epiphany, Presentation in the Temple, our Lord's fast, the Passion and Resurrection, etc.—they all form a unique cycle. It is like a unique
celebration reaching its climax or innermost center by means
of preparation and successive stages. Christmas, Epiphany and
our Lord's fast find their whole meaning in Easter, the mystery of death inseparable from the mystery of new life. Whatever the feast, it is always the celebration of the Covenant,
whose sacrament is the Mass, the heart of all the feasts, which
is also the memorial of the Lord's Pasch.

The liturgy adds a sanctoral cycle to its temporal one,
because it never separates the Body from the Head, the
saints from their Lord and Master. In the celebration of the
liturgy the whole mystical vine of salvation is communicated. It is truly the total reality of the Covenant that is
offered to us.

It is not only taught to us or merely brought to our
notice; it is celebrated, realized, rendered present and communicated, not simply as a doctrine and truth, but as a
reality. The doctrinal feasts were instituted relatively recently.
They have a lot to recommend them, but even before the
institution of a feast of Christ the King the liturgy was
from beginning to end, and still is, the very realization and
proclamation of the universal Lordship of Christ; it taught

and teaches this by all that it is; it brings home this truth in a living way, exactly as a family inculcates the sense of duty in a child without giving him theoretical lessons on the subject. There was talk of instituting a feast of the Redemption! It is unlikely that this will happen, and it would be quite superfluous if proper use is made of the liturgy, because the liturgy is, from beginning to end, the active celebration of the Redemption, and its efficacious enactment.[6] The liturgy does not theorize on the Redemption, but it ceaselessly brings us into loving communication with Christ our Savior, with his Cross and its fruit, the hope of eternal life. Similarly, to return to the second example given in chapter one, the liturgy teaches scarcely any lessons about the Eucharist—and none before the institution of the feast of Corpus Christi in 1264. But the liturgy celebrates the Eucharist; it offers us the means by which we may prepare ourselves to approach it; the liturgy brings us into communication with it and envelops it in a whole cult and worship, which radiates naturally from it.

As action, actual celebration and ritual, the liturgy has an exceptional richness and comprehensiveness. A text, however rich, always expresses the limits of its author's thought and of the means of communication employed. But above all, only a portion of a text's content is ever assimilated, and this is even true of the biblical text, whose richness is immense

---

[6] The Secret for the 9th Sunday after Pentecost can never be quoted too often: "... *quia quoties hujus hostiae commemoratio celebratur, opus nostrae redemptionis exercetur.*" "For each and every offering of this memorial sacrifice carries on the work of our redemption." [This Latin prayer is now part of the Prayer over the Gifts, Second Sunday in Ordinary Time. The ICEL translation for this prayer reads, "Father, may we celebrate the eucharist with reverence and love, for when we proclaim the death of the Lord you continue the work of his redemption ...—ED.]

since its principal author is the Holy Spirit. A definition narrows down reality; and the intellect narrows down the definition.

An action, on the contrary, creates a synthesis. The celebration of the Eucharist communicates the *whole* reality; the merest sign of the cross is an entire profession of faith in the Redemption. In the middle of the fourth century, St. Hilary said that the whole Trinitarian doctrine was delivered and contained in baptism, with the efficacy of the words by which it is administered.[7] Here the rite itself is a wonderful guardian of the fullness of the deposit; it remains intact through all the surrounding changes. Certain realities may have been criticized, opposed or forgotten; their meaning may have been lost: but they were preserved by the rite, in spite of this, and, seen under a new light, in happier surroundings, they could be rediscovered intact, in their unchanging and somewhat old-fashioned setting. At certain periods, for example, a real understanding of the Mass had been obscured; in others, had the movement of historical criticism been followed, nothing would have remained of the episcopacy. It is thanks to the rite that the present-day liturgical and ecclesiological movement is rediscovering intact, treasures misunderstood in the past.

It is true that the liturgical rite also has its dangers. It is wholly concerned with the spirit, on which all its value depends, for if it is not informed by the spirit it may become a meaningless practice or a strict conservatism preventing growth and life. But, as originally inspired, it is the body in which the spirit is preserved, and when the spirit reawakens, it also comes to life, kept intact in its totality.

This aspect of totality that characterizes both the liturgy and tradition, for the same reasons, is also found in the admirable

---

[7] *De Trinitate*, lib. 2, c. 1 (PL 10:50).

comprehensiveness of the liturgy, which unifies and harmonizes elements often separated and even placed in opposition to one another. It unifies the most personal values with the most communal, the most tangible realities with the most spiritual, discipline or ritualism with inner feelings or inspiration, the hierarchic structure with popular expression, the priesthood of the ministry with the consecrated state of the whole body of the faithful, and so on.

Nothing is more educative for man in his totality than the liturgy. The Bible is certainly a marvelous teacher of prayer, of the sense of God and of the adult convictions of conscience. Used alone, the Bible might produce a Christian of the Puritan tradition, an individualist and even a visionary. The liturgy, however, is "the authentic method instituted by the Church to unite souls to Jesus".[8] The sort of Christian produced by an enlightened and docile participation in the liturgy is a man at peace and unified in every fiber of his human nature, by the secret and powerful penetration of faith and love in his life, throughout a period of prayer and worship, during which he learned, at his mother's knee and without effort, *the Church's language*: her language of faith, love, hope and fidelity. There is no better way of acquiring "the mind of the Church" in the widest and most interior interpretation of this expression; it is something quite different from an instinctive obedience. It concerns the delicate inner feeling that unites us to the thought and feelings of Christ's Bride. There are certain comparisons and conceptions that are made possible only by maintaining a spiritual contact with a given object and by returning to what it represents, motivated by love. This is what Mary did with regard to Jesus, as St. Luke testifies (Lk 2:19, 51); and it is what the Church

[8] Dom Festugière, *La Liturgie catholique* (Maredsous, 1913), p. 119.

does ceaselessly, as "the Mary of the history of the world" (H. Rahner). Like the liturgy, tradition is the action of a subject who loves, prays, meditates and, in so doing, progressively reaches a deeper understanding of what it holds and practices each day.

b. The liturgy as the essential transmission of something not contained formally in Scripture

The Scriptures do not express everything entrusted by Christ to the Church for us to live by, even though, according to an opinion common to the Fathers and to the Middle Ages, they contain all the truths necessary for salvation. However providential the recording of the apostolic writings might be, at the time they were the reply to given circumstances. As we have seen, had it not been for the defects in the celebration of the Eucharist at Corinth, we should not have St. Paul's important text on the mystery of the Body and Blood, and the critics would not have failed to say that this mystery was unknown to Paul, and so on.

The liturgy provides a contact with the realities themselves, even though this contact is not as immediate as that resulting from a total experience. It is thus, for example, that the communion of saints, kept in the memory of the faithful, has led them to recognize the legitimacy of a certain devotion, of a recourse to their intercession, and finally to a veneration of their images, leading to a certain practice of the remission of temporal punishment or indulgences: these are so many points not formally attested in the Scriptures, although the foundation or indications of them are found there, or at least their basic principle (in the idea of the Mystical Body and the communion of saints). In this case it is surely unnecessary to resort to the theory of traditions that were purely oral, though comprising formal declarations (*locu-tio formalis*), as did certain Fathers and medieval theologians. All this can be said to reside in tradition, without imagining a sort of whispered transmission from mouth to mouth, coming from Christ and traversing the centuries outside all written attestation, which seems an easy way out and most unlikely. Living tradition, faithfully lived by Christians, is not creative, but it is, in a sense, a source of Revelation—precisely because it contains and makes explicit things that it has always held and practiced concretely, but for which, in the beginning, there existed no written or verbal formulation. Is this not so in our everyday experience? The conscience and its real content cannot be identified with its subsequent expression, which remains fragmentary.

Similar explanations could be given regarding the Virgin Mary, Mother of Jesus Christ. Before the institution of the liturgical feasts transforming the Church's belief ("doxologically") into praise, this belief had been recognized and stated, taking its origin in the spiritual experience of the devotion of the faithful, all-embracing to begin with, but rich in meaning. This is the actual course taken by the doctrines of the Assumption and the Immaculate Conception of the Mother of God. Once again, it is chiefly in this sense that they are said to be contained in tradition. This is reason enough to make it clear that tradition should not be identified with its formal expression or its monuments.

c. The liturgy as an interpretation of the holy Scriptures that brings home their meaning

The liturgy is interwoven, so to speak, with texts from the holy Scriptures. The faithful are aware of this, especially those who have known the happy change brought about in their Christian outlook and way of life by following Mass regularly and attentively in a good Missal. It is true that they are sometimes a little put off by certain texts, or by the application of these to episodes or individuals that the texts certainly do not concern, taken in the literal and historical sense: for example, certain texts from the Book of Wisdom or from the Song of Songs applied to the Virgin Mary; at times the verse chosen for the feast of a given saint appears to rely on a play on words or a subtle interpretation. On the other hand, the liturgy often links things in a striking way; for a certain feast it manages to choose psalms, passages from the prophets or accounts that do not spring to mind and that show how the main elements of the Christian mystery are prefigured in the Old Testament and are like recurring themes in God's plan. For the religious soul this is a source of joy for the spirit, bringing an expansive certainty, peace and an abundance of spiritual nourishment. At other times, the link forged between a text or episode from the Old Testament and a text or story from the New is as much a contrast as a sign of continuity. Two episodes are placed side by side to show that the Old Testament is fulfilled by the New, but it is a fulfillment that often exceeds our expectations. A particularly good example of this is found in the sequence of ferial (that is, weekday) Masses during Lent. Moreover, the liturgy reveals once again its conformity with early Christian art; whether it be in the catacombs or the mosaics (those, for example, of St. Mary Major, in Rome), or in the stained glass and sculptures of our cathedrals, scenes from the Old Testament are continually compared and contrasted with episodes from the New. This was one of the most common methods of early catechetics. It abounds in the preaching of the Fathers, also in the liturgy and artistic representations, and is consonant with the very spirit of tradition considered as an interpretation of the holy Scriptures, centered on Christ and the Church.

Like the Scriptures, the liturgy is both centered on Christ and totally directed toward God; it has the same preoccupation with the history of salvation as the Bible, but, being enacted in the light of the events of Easter and Pentecost, it highlights more clearly the major figures and principal features of this history. It renders the Christological sense of the whole Bible more explicit. Jesus said: "If you believed Moses, you would believe me, for he wrote of me." [9] On the evening of Easter, he explained the Scriptures to his apostles with reference to the central mystery of his own Pasch (cf. Lk 24:25–27, 44–46). The liturgy has inherited the information he communicated to his disciples. Its manner of quoting and interpreting the texts is consonant and in agreement with that of the Fathers, of the apostles and of Jesus himself: and like this last it is typological. It seeks its norms of action in the major and unchanging principles of God's action, among the examples that reveal his mode of action, presented throughout the whole of sacred history and the Scriptures. [10] Thus, if tradition in its dogmatic foundation is an interpretation of Scripture continuing that of Christ and the apostles, the liturgy is truly the holy ark containing sacred tradition at its most intense. It communicates the spirit of Christ as the radiant center of the whole history of salvation without ever separating him from the Church and the saints, which are his field of influence. And it does so, not so much by learned instruction as by realizing the mystery of Christ

[9] Jn 5:46; cf. 1:45; 2:22; 5:38–39; 12:16, 41; 19:28; 20:9.

[10] See EH, pp. 76–91, which shows that such was the exegetical method of the Fathers and of the New Testament itself.

concretely, here and now, by celebrating and almost acting it, returning to it ceaselessly to illuminate it, like the sun, which shines on a beautiful landscape successively from different viewpoints and with a varying intensity of light: "We need to assimilate things slowly, rather than their explanations." [11]

THE FATHERS OF THE CHURCH

Many of the faithful imagine the strangest things when a preacher rashly alludes to "the Fathers of the Church" in a sermon: they picture a collection of ancestors, or even a group of respectable personalities of the present day. Many imagine nothing at all; for them the expression is devoid of meaning. The better informed know that the name "Fathers" refers to writers who were also saints, and usually bishops, who, at a time when it was necessary to provide some foundation for Catholic thought, preached the Church's doctrine, elaborated it, defended it and defined it against heresy.

This general idea is correct, but it needs a more accurate definition. St. Jerome (d. 420), who is one of the Fathers, already employed another and wider category, namely, that of "ecclesiastical writers". Not all the great minds who lived, preached and wrote during the above-mentioned period merit the name of "Father", however great their genius. Tertullian, for example (d. after 220), exerted a great influence over Latin theology, whose language he was largely responsible for creating; but he fell into the Montanist heresy. He was an ecclesiastical writer of the first order, but not a Father of the Church. Origen, his junior by a few years (d. 254), was one of the most brilliant minds of the whole of Christian history.

---

[11] Fr. Duployé, in *Maison-Dieu*, no. 10 (1947), p. 43.

With a soul of fire and filled with love for God and Jesus Christ, he professed the faith during persecutions. He lacked dependability and a certain balance of thought, which prevents him from being fully counted among the Fathers of the Church. He was almost too brilliant, too original and too personal.

The Fathers sought, not so much to exercise their genius, as to serve, express, defend and illustrate the common faith. This is undoubtedly why they are termed "the Fathers", as though the Church was not so much indebted to their individual talent as to their corporate contribution as such. In any case, in giving them this title, she not only considers the outstanding quality of the doctrine, but also its orthodoxy. The category of "ecclesiastical writers" is purely historical and literary; that of "Fathers" is dogmatic and implies a judgment of value whose basis is not purely historical or scientific, but doctrinal. This means, finally, that the Fathers of the Church are those whom the Church herself recognizes as such.

What is meant by the Church? Each time the word "Church" is used we should imagine the whole community of Christians, forming an organically structured body, all of whose parts are living but do not all carry out the same functions. Certain of them have a function of government. The Catholic spirit of the whole body is the first to discern the doctrines, but the Magisterium completes it. It is the latter, the "teaching Church", which finally judges the orthodoxy of the doctrine and recognizes in the holy Doctors this authority whose conditions I have tried to define. It is equally necessary to define its limits.

It is generally agreed that the age of the Fathers ends at the boundary of the sixth and seventh centuries for the West, with St. Gregory the Great (d. 604) and St. Isidore of Seville

(d. 636), and at the death of St. John Damascene, for the East (c. 749). This chronological limit is naturally questionable, but there are good reasons for it, based on the historical role played by the Fathers, a role that can be explained as follows: the Christians who lived at the time of the great persecutions had known an atmosphere of opposition to the world, remaining fairly alien to its development and the main realities of political life and largely passive in the cultural domain, with which they had little to do; they were not opposed to it, but indifferent rather, all their attention being turned toward the Kingdom that was to come. After the peace of Constantine (313), Christianity was forced to take its place in public life, where it was honored and favored. There it met widely with a literary and philosophical culture still very much alive, in the tradition of the pagan authors. From that time the Church simultaneously encountered two closely linked and similar risks: that of becoming worldly, owing to the support of the secular power and her union with it; and that of becoming hesitant and somewhat syncretist with regard to doctrine, owing to the contact, and even exchange, with pagan forms of thought and worship, various elements of which were taken over.

When one studies a chronological table showing the literary activity of Christian writers decade by decade, and almost year by year, one is struck forcibly to see, after the nearly empty second and third centuries, how the columns suddenly fill between the mid-fourth century and the middle of the fifth. The names and the works proliferate: the greatest names and the most decisive works—Basil, Gregory of Nyssa, Gregory of Nazianzus, Jerome, Ambrose, John Chrysostom, Augustine, Cyril of Alexandria, Leo. It is the golden age of the Fathers. Their vocation and particular task, for which they received a corresponding grace, was to mold the spiritual life and thought of the Church in a society whose culture derived from a pagan tradition; to put at the disposal of the faith a political power and philosophical defense, which was to constitute a danger for her, maintaining nonetheless the purity of Christianity's own inspiration, as well as its demands. This task was to come to an end in the West when the Empire was overwhelmed by barbarian invasions, its political power shattered and its philosophical, scientific and academic traditions suspended. It is true that other tasks then presented themselves, just as new duties have constantly made themselves felt to the Church throughout the centuries. She was subsequently destined to "pass into the hands of the barbarians", and she has never ceased to be solicited by new "barbarians", presented to her by each age to evangelize and baptize. A similar constellation of geniuses and saints, called upon to define the Church's belief in its essential principles, was not to be repeated in the history of Christian thought.

This is why, even if in one sense the Fathers represent a historical moment in the life of the Church that should not be exaggerated to the detriment of other equally important and valuable moments, in another sense they represent a unique moment, forever decisive and exemplary. We must not, however, put the Fathers on a pedestal in an idealistic and somewhat false golden age that has gone forever: the Spirit is still at work in the Church, and he is not absent from our own age. To treat the age of the Fathers as an absolute would be to deny the possibility of new adaptations of any depth with regard to new cultures, when in our time so many nations in the East, in Africa and South America—not to speak of the new technological world—are knocking at the Church's doors. And yet, however receptive she may be to new forms of humanity, the Church has already fixed her own temperament in relation to the basic intellectual options at this historical moment of her life, when men who were both geniuses and saints were providentially given to her in abundance. A country's civilization benefits ceaselessly from new creative influences—and yet it usually takes as reference a classical period when the fundamental characteristics of its genius were expressed vigorously, simply and entirely centered on the essentials. Similarly, in each of our lives there exists a time when, leaving childhood behind, we reveal the outline of our moral and intellectual character, largely as a result of meeting something new, or in reaction to something we reject. The Church had her classical period during the fourth and fifth centuries, during which, by the battles of the Fathers and the great Councils, she defined her faith in the face of the Trinitarian and Christological heresies, in other words, on the most fundamental and essential questions; during which the texts of the great liturgies were composed, after a period of creative freedom[12]; during which the first religious rules and the conciliar canons laid the foundation of canonical and ascetic legislation, with the result that whatever has been created and experienced since has benefited from the contribution of the Fathers and is measured by it, albeit unconsciously. Every Christian believes in the holy Trinity with the Council of Nicaea and with St. Athanasius, who defended it heroically and lucidly. Every Christian believes in the personal divinity of the Holy Spirit with the Council of Constantinople of 381 and with St. Basil, who prepared the definition. Every believer who participates in the eucharistic liturgy prays with those who formulated it, starting from the middle

[12] In the East, the classical anaphoras were fixed in the fourth century: that of the *Apostolic Constitutions* and those that bear the names of the great doctors: anaphora of St. Basil, of St. Gregory of Nazianzus, of St. Cyril, and even, in its primitive Antiochian form, that of St. John Chrysostom.

of the fourth century. Every monk is dependent on St. Pacho-
mius, St. Basil and St. Benedict.

It is this line of reasoning that explains the title of "Fathers",
in the extension as well as the precision of its meaning. Those
who deserve this title were sons of the Church; they themselves claimed to have contributed nothing besides that which
they had received, and thus to be men of tradition, in the
ordinary sense of the word. Their statements to this effect
are innumerable. But they were also really her Fathers (and
ours) in that, in a certain way, they engendered the Church,
not by giving birth to her, like her founders or first progen-
itors, but by contributing to her life, her genius and her temperament a few of the fundamental characteristics that fixed
her image. In this sense, their thought, their activity and their
creations were "exemplary" and serve as a reference, consciously or subconsciously, in the same way that a live being
is measured against its "type", not mechanically, however,
which would be a simple imitation, but in a living and creative way that is free in its very docility.

In order to play this role, by a special favor the Fathers
were endowed with a genius, which I should like to examine briefly and which is very familiar to the diligent reader
of their works.

The Fathers are first and foremost commentators of the
holy Scriptures. The treatises in which St. Athanasius questions the arguments of the Arians are nothing more than a
commentary on the basic verses of Scripture, or those that
are the object of controversy. The Rules of St. Basil are interwoven with scriptural texts. St. Augustine preached his finest series of sermons in the form of a commentary verse by
verse on the Psalms and on St. John. This patristic writing
is also clearly pastoral, which explains its vigor and
straightforwardness, characteristic of Church writing. For this

very reason the Fathers introduced few subtle or unusual questions in their dogmatic writing, contenting themselves with a systematic investigation; but this does not mean that they abstained from the most profound meditations—take St. Augustine's *De Trinitate*, for example. As a result of all this, and also because the Fathers' attitude was wholly spiritual, their writing, when compared with the Christian reality, reveals an immediacy that brings it close to the simple and vigorous text of the witnesses. Living with Scripture and nourished by it, when faced with the first heresies attacking the foundations of the faith, the Fathers concentrated their reflection on the essentials. They avoided introducing human and specific research into their teaching and never lost sight of the totality of the faith, united as it is by its center, namely, the Christian mystery, and converging toward its object, our union with God. From beginning to end the Fathers are concerned entirely with the mystery of Christ, God made man to restore creation's true meaning according to God and to bring man into communion with the divine life, to which he is destined and called by God. This is why, by always concentrating on the whole and on its center, the Fathers bring the whole to life in each of its parts. They do not speak of Christ without speaking of the Church, nor of baptism or the Eucharist without showing the totality of the mystery of our Redemption and of our introduction into the divine life. With them everything has its place in the harmony.

The Fathers are men of unity; this is apparent in their lives and in their writing. With them there is no separation between ascesis and theology, or between the life of prayer and the speculative contemplation of the mysteries. Often having come from monachism, they are the best examples of the ideal of a unified and fully integrated humanity, which is the model of Christian anthropology.

They also succeed wonderfully in communicating a sense of its totality, centered on Jesus Christ, who is the principle itself of this Christological, anthropological and cosmic interpretation of the holy Scriptures, of which tradition is composed in its main dogmatic aspect. Their *ethos*, climate of thought and view of things are the actual *ethos*, climate and view of the Bible. They share its conception of the history of the world and of man, and of the history of salvation.

All this explains why they are favored witnesses of tradition, whose spirit radiates and is absorbed from them; through them the influence of tradition is felt.

This does not mean that *everything* they say is to be accepted as the actual expression of *the* tradition. They are its favored witnesses and not purely and simply the tradition. There are even errors here and there in the writing of the greatest among them: St. Irenaeus shared in the millennial theories of his time; St. Augustine, in his fight against the Pelagians, overexaggerated a pessimistic view of human effort; many of the Trinitarian definitions of the pre-Nicaean Fathers are insufficient or debatable. The treatises of theological criteriology teach that the Fathers form an absolutely valid reference in matters of faith only when their teaching is unanimous and claims to be the faith of the Church. The treatises say the same thing of the theologians and even of the ordinary Magisterium of the bishops. They have elaborated a whole system to determine the different degrees of certainty in the use of these secondary theological sources. These details are so many different ways in which tradition is separated from its monuments or witnesses. This matter concerning the witnesses or monuments is very important and will be examined in the second half of this chapter.

TRADITION AND ITS MONUMENTS:
CONTINUITY AND SEPARATION

The following expression is often found in theological manuals: a certain point of doctrine is "proved by tradition", *probatur ex traditione*. It is followed by three or four passages from the Fathers and sometimes, though rarely, by a reference to the liturgy or early Christian art. A more accurate expression of this idea would be the following: this point belongs to the tradition of the Church, which can be shown by the monuments or witnesses of this tradition. In fact, the monuments of tradition are not tradition itself, which transcends them; they are the concrete expression of various aspects of it and thus, for us, a means of reaching this tradition and identifying it.

Historians are apt to identify tradition with what is accessible from documents of the past, thus reducing the content of present-day tradition to that which can be supported by documentary evidence, and they oppose progress and adaptation in the name of fidelity to the past. There were traces of this in the attitude of the Gallicans, well versed in the history of the Church's "police" activities, and in that of the Jansenists, specialists in the matter of Christian discipline. It was apparent in Ignatius Döllinger's attitude in refusing to accept the dogmas promulgated by the First Vatican Council in 1870, in the name of history. It was apparent in many Protestant reactions to the dogmatic definition of the Assumption of the Blessed Virgin Mary, when they pointed out that such a belief could not belong to the deposit of Revelation since it lacked not only biblical support but also authentic testimony before the middle of the fourth century. Even in the Catholic Church, a patrologist as eminent as B. Altaner was of the opinion, for the same reason, that this belief could not be "defined" as belonging to divine faith.

I can understand the uneasiness felt by a historian faced with an excessive disparity between the documents and the pronouncements. I shall soon discuss the place and indispensable role of documentary evidence, but it is first necessary to show that tradition is not limited to the documents. This results from its nature. Indeed, by its very nature tradition contains a living subject among the elements that constitute it. We know what this subject is: on the higher, transcendent level it is the Holy Spirit, who guarantees the unity of our knowledge of the faith, despite the variations and the distance of space and time; on the visible and historical level it is the Church, a body wholly animated by faith, with its Magisterium, which receives assistance to preach, keep, explain and define this faith authentically.

The Church lives on the deposit; the Magisterium receives assistance *only* to keep and explain the deposit. Neither the Church nor the Magisterium has the slightest autonomy with regard to the deposit, and it is to it alone that they owe their life and even existence. But the deposit itself, exactly like the Revelation, whose name refers to the same reality but from its aspect of knowledge, is not reduced to *statements*, or formal expressions, as the Scholastics would say; it also comprises *realities*, which form part of the Church's historical life: the reality of the sacraments, of the Lord's presence in the Eucharist and by his Spirit, of the indwelling of the Blessed Trinity in the soul, of the communion of saints and the assistance of their prayers, etc. We have seen, with the help of Maurice Blondel, that these realities in the Church are the elements of a spiritual experience by which she can understand things really contained in the deposit, but which the *texts* do not express formally. By meditating on the texts and events, by examining the implications of her experience of the sacred truths she possesses, by rereading the texts once more in the light of this experience, the Church gradually recognizes in the divine Word a richer content than that which had been revealed by a merely historical interpretation of the texts alone. Those who wish to know nothing but the text, and to limit themselves to a scientific interpretation, will not reach this level. On the other hand, the Church reaches this level, as the actual level of her tradition, when she summons the resources of her inner experience, of her reflection, of the "meditation in her heart" made by the Church, following the example of the Virgin Mary (Lk 2:19, 51), going beyond the historical and philological resources, which do not amount to very much. In her tradition the Church behaves according to her nature, which is different from that of history: she is a nation of believers, a communion of saints, a Magisterium that receives guidance, an inheritor of the apostles' mission to spread the Gospel. From this point of view the testimony God has committed to the scriptural texts is understood in the light of the event, a little as God's testimony in the Old Testament concerning the Messiah was understood by the disciples in the light of Christ's advent and of his Pasch.[13] By the guidance of the Holy Spirit given to the whole Church, and especially to her Magisterium, it becomes a living witness of God. This is the Church's life of faith.

It is evident that the Church has no autonomy with regard to the deposit, but she is not tied within strict limits to the testimony contained in the monuments of her tradition. Tradition transcends them as well as being contained by them. The monuments express it and in this sense contain it, but it

---

[13] See Lk 24:25–27, 44 ff.; and p. 142, n. 10, above.

goes beyond them and is not limited to them: a little as an event is always more than the account of it given by a witness or, better still, as awareness of something is more than its expression. Tradition is like the Church's awareness; it cannot be limited to what has been expressed by certain people in the past.

Thus it becomes clear that it is not the historian's task to judge the Church's tradition in the final instance: it is the task of the Church herself and of her Magisterium. Those who regard tradition as almost entirely confined to documents and neglect its vital elements—the believing Church, the teaching Church and the Holy Spirit, who supports and enlightens them—tend, at least in practice, to ascribe a teaching authority to the Doctors and universities. Catholic theology, on the other hand, in the nineteenth century and especially at the beginning of the twentieth, influenced either by the development of the Marian dogmas or by the Modernist crisis, has come to distinguish between historical or documentary tradition, which is the study of those expert in ancient documents, and theological or dogmatic tradition, which is the study of the *Church* and which only she can judge.

This distinction is well founded and very important. But if it should be taken seriously at a theological level, it is equally important to avoid using it superficially and underestimating the importance of documents as witnesses of tradition and the means of reaching it. Indeed, the Church invents nothing; she receives no new Revelation to alter or enrich the object of the saving faith. She is linked to the deposit in the same way that she is necessarily apostolic. Her hierarchy is assisted with the sole object of being totally the witness and guardian of this deposit. She must therefore take positive nourishment from the revealed message. It is obvious that the documents that expressed this message at the beginning, and continuously through the centuries since then, are a special means of knowing what has always been believed and what was delivered in the first place. With regard to this beginning, the apostolic documents, that is, the writings of the New Testament, constitute an unparalleled source of knowledge. Their value is absolute and unquestionable, at least from a negative point of view, in that whatever is contradicted by them definitely and without question could not belong to the revealed deposit. Thus, in a wider setting than its role as nourishment for the faith and sacrament of salvation by faith, Scripture plays a critical role with regard to every affirmation claimed within the Church. It is the comprehensive rule to which all preaching, worship, devotion and doctrinal development should be referred. With certain reservations, a similar judgment could be passed on the other monuments of tradition: the liturgy, the writings of the Fathers, the early canons and constitutions, all different expressions of the Church's faith. The purely dogmatic texts enjoy a favored position, as has been said; the others represent a whole scale of authority: but at a deeper level than their semijuridical application, they represent, fixed once and for all, a mirror revealing the image of the early Church, whose faithful descendants we are, or strive to be.

CONCLUSION:
TRADITION AT THE CENTER
OF THE CHURCH

We have, I trust, recognized the greatness of tradition. Taken in its widest sense, it was seen to occupy a central position in the Church. In a sense it is her life itself, or, if you prefer, the nourishment of that life. As such it is *received*. Everything in the Church comes from elsewhere, from certain sources that are the fountainheads of the history of salvation. Christianity is essentially an inheritance, passed down by our Fathers in the faith. But tradition is also present today. Age-old, it is ever fresh and alive; using its inherited riches, it answers the unexpected questions of today. It advances through history toward its final consummation, its development coinciding with that of believing and Christian humanity itself. It is borne by living men who succeed one another, and at the same time it is borne within them by a subject who transcends them: the Holy Spirit, the principle of communion, who effects the Church's unity throughout time as well as space.

There is tradition and there are traditions. The latter are ways of living and expressing the faith: customs, rites, practical methods and all kinds of concrete details, which have also been passed on, forming a certain system of discipline for the Christian life. They cannot be completely justified, either by the original texts, the holy Scriptures in particular, or by decisive arguments. They are capital, however, in the conservation of Christianity's vitality. They represent for it notably what a language represents for a given national culture: the concrete carrier of a spirit, that which enables one to become an actual member of a certain community, by receiving, effortlessly and almost unconsciously, a certain type of humanity. To receive and keep the traditions is to learn the Catholic language of the Fathers and Ancients. In their small way these traditions also lend a certain warmth, without which our Church would be more like an old-fashioned classroom than a home. They create this warm atmosphere of familiarity and security that belongs to a house that is lived in, to a home. And yet, they have not the same absolute value as the tradition of the faith; they are rather tradition's external form.

As with the Church, one can only speak dialectically of tradition, making contrary statements about it, which are, however, true simultaneously. To say that it is at the center of Catholicism or Christianity means that it shares the same paradoxes and tensions. It is necessary to mention only the greatest of these tensions to see how aptly they describe the very essence of tradition.

"It is well known", said Lacordaire in his thirty-first Conference at Notre-Dame (1845), "that distance destroys unity." How is it that what appeared once, in a given place and in a definite form, can be communicated so as to be held and lived everywhere, by a great number of people and under such novel conditions, without losing its original identity? How can Jerusalem become the world? Will not the rigidity of structure of a deposit laid down once and for all prevent its content from being presented in a way that is up to date and active throughout the world's history? Tradition fulfills these conditions. It is both changeless and up to date, a reminder of past events and the presentation of their significance, conforming with what has been laid down once and for all and presenting this very message in a way that is always relevant and dynamic. It brings up to date and communicates the unique source.

Tradition is equally continuity and progress, conservation and development. Two dangers threaten it, however: that of remaining static and depending too much on the forms handed down from the past, and that of remaining too independent of the advance of new ideas and of their general acceptance. In this matter of conservatism many identify tradition with "accepted ideas"[1] or call "traditional" things of yesteryear. Most of the present [1964] "traditions" of our parishes and ecclesiastical life date from the nineteenth century. On the contrary, as we have seen, the real reform is an appeal made by a shallower tradition to a more profound one; it is a return to the principle itself whose recent expression or realization is alone questioned and judged obsolete because it is inadequate or has strayed too far from the original meaning of the profound principle, which needs to be paid greater respect. Minds are often divided into two categories—conservative and progressive—but experience shows that the same men can be ultraconservative on certain matters and adventurous or progressive on others, above all because many men adopt a position less as a result of a coherent and reasoned criticism of the truth than from sentimental reasons that lead them sometimes to the right and sometimes to the left.

While it is extension and progress, tradition remains linked to its roots. The Holy Spirit is the divine guarantee of its fidelity. Catholic theology has never ceased to proclaim this;

[1] See my *Vraie et fausse réforme dans l'Église* (Paris, 1950), pp. 315 ff. and 532 ff.

its doctrine of tradition would be meaningless and inconstant if the Holy Spirit's action, promised to the Church, and his role were not stressed as much as they are. But tradition, which is thus a life force and therefore interior or immanent, is also linked to a deposit having its external forms or witnesses. We have studied the monuments of tradition and have spoken of the Scriptures, the memorial of the interventions made by God in order to found his People, coming to us through his prophets, through Jesus Christ and his apostles.

The interior quality of the life that the Spirit gives the Church does not prevent her from being *tied* to this testimony and having to refer to it as an ever-valid rule of her conscience and life. The entire history of the Church is characterized by a tension between an ideal of *plenitude* and an ideal of *purity*.[2] The former leads her to seek breadth of vision, a receptive attitude and progress, and to make a synthesis of what she encounters, but it brings with it a risk of loss of purity. The latter must ceaselessly repeat its demands, in the name of the original principles, to which the holy Scriptures bear the most constant, complete and undeniable witness. This is why Scripture is a necessary critical reference for any development or growth of tradition.[3]

[2] For the questions raised here, see J. M. Paupert, *What Is the Gospel?* (New York: Hawthorn Books, 1962).

[3] E. Ortigues, in "La tradition de l'Évangile dans l'Église, d'après la tradition catholique", *Foi et Vie* (July 1951), pp. 304–22 and 316–17, expresses this well when he writes: "The function of Tradition is to make us *share* in the fellowship of the Spirit of Jesus Christ, in the faith. It is a means of participation in the Body of Christ, that is, in the Church's sacramental structure, the word 'sacramental' here signifying, in the wide sense, the sign through which the Holy Spirit enlightens us by uniting us. Scripture's task is to confront us with the testimony of the prophets and apostles to remind us that the Word of God is an initiative that does not allow itself to be absorbed by

The Reformation, not only in its original requests, which were largely ignored, but also in its permanent position next to the ancient Church, is certainly an important safeguard to prevent us from paying too little attention to the demands of this critical reference. Its profound plea, in fact, consists in reminding the Church that, even with the Holy Spirit dwelling in her, she does not possess her norm within herself, for this would amount to setting up her own life as the norm of this selfsame life; she receives only the Spirit, who dwells in her in order to develop, in an interior and living manner, the life given to her once and for all by the prophets, the apostles and the Lord Jesus, this "faith which was once for all delivered to the saints", of which St. Jude's epistle speaks (v. 3). The Church's fidelity to her Lord demands not only that she listen to him within herself, in her own conscience, but also as the voice of Another, her Master.

The importance of what was at stake in the controversy in which the Reformers were engaged with the ancient Church becomes apparent. The debate has been going on for more than four centuries now, and it is not over yet. The criticisms and denials aimed by the sixteenth-century Reformers at tradition have succeeded neither in excluding nor even in disqualifying this tradition. But on the other hand, the replies from the Catholic side to this criticism have not succeeded in abolishing the protest. Are we destined to remain eternally at the same stage in the controversy?

---

the community, but takes the form of an ever-present dialogue. Scripture's task is to bring preaching constantly back to the unity of this divine initiative; it is the inspired instrument of the analogy of faith, that is, the permanent re-centering of the faith on the essential elements of this dialogue, the redemptive Revelation."

THE PROBLEM OF TRADITION TODAY

The opposition between Protestantism on the one hand and the ancient Church (Catholicism and Eastern Orthodoxy, equally in this matter) on the other is certainly very deep. It concerns the question of a norm *for the Church*, in the sense that has just been described, and the question of discovering what is the norm for each believer, thus concerning the true nature and authentic foundation of the religious relationship. As we have already said, the question is to know whether the Church instituted by God, with its hierarchic structure of Magisterium and priesthood, constitutes an essential element of the religious relationship, or whether this relationship is established directly and on a personal level between man and God. In this case no authority would intervene other than that of *God* in person, expressing himself by his Word, that is, concretely, in the Scriptures.

But how does Scripture—these writings and no others—come to be recognized as the Word of God? On its own merits? How can we be sure of understanding Scripture correctly? By its own coherence and self-defense? How do all believers achieve St. Paul's wish that "there be no dissentions among you, but that you be united in the same mind and the same judgment" (1 Cor 1:10)? By means of an inner and personal determination that makes everyone read the same texts in the same way?

It is superfluous here either to describe or to justify the traditional position, which holds that God has not only supplied us with his written Word from without to unite us to him in a single fellowship of faith, and placed his Spirit within each of us, but has also supplied us with a public institution, common to all and assisted as such by the Holy Spirit, whose authority is of a nature equal to that of God's Word, even though it is tied to the latter and subordinated to it. Moreover, this institution is not simply a "system"; it is a fount of grace and a fellowship. As such it is, above all, the setting for a spiritual experience by which this institution learns continually about the content and meaning of the heritage by which it lives. As such it is also a fraternity, a family: the communion of saints, dare we say, in which nothing is lost, each benefiting from all the others and from a treasury amassed through the centuries by the active contribution of all, and of those in particular whom God has especially gifted.

But, during the last twenty years [1944–1964] in particular, there has been a change in the world of disunited Christians. There are the movements resulting from individual causes within each of the churches; but no church today is entirely independent of the movements of the whole Christian world, or even of those of the world itself. The ecumenical movement has become so important and widespread that it has created a new climate in which the churches live even their own inner lives and in which nearly all the theological problems that still separate them can be approached in a renewed manner, which is both more constructive and full of promise. Everywhere a renewal of the very idea of a Church is also noticeable, a movement, eventually converging, that will lead to a fuller understanding of her true nature and authentic composition. As Dr. Dibelius stated in 1926, the twentieth century may well be "the century of the Church".

This process of ecclesiological rediscovery has been very active in the Catholic Church, and, indeed, her last word on the matter has not yet been said.[4] We have also been

---

[4] I have traced this activity in many periodicals and reviews, which are presented collectively in *Sainte Église: Études et approches ecclésiologiques* (Paris: Cerf, 1963).

witnessing, for some time now, beginning in about 1937 or 1938, a widespread renewal of patristic studies and a powerful biblical movement. All of this is bound to lead to a greater comprehension of tradition and of its relationship with the Church and with Scripture: three inseparable realities that a truly Catholic theology succeeds precisely in uniting and linking together. In this domain, as in so many others, there are signs that we are overcoming a certain narrowness of outlook and rigidity left by the Counter-Reformation. It is thus, for example, that the question of the relationship between Scripture and tradition can no longer be stated simply in terms of competition, as though the one supplies what the other does not contain materially. In my opinion, Professor J. R. Geiselmann's otherwise valuable and acceptable contribution is limited by the fact that in stating the question (to which he offers a solution quite different from that of the Counter-Reformation) he does not free himself sufficiently from the old way of stating the problem, by a wider, more positive and constructive approach with regard to the inner originality of tradition.

The attitude of the Reformers to tradition was one of polemic, opposition and refusal; it is even debatable whether they really tackled the question of *the* tradition. In the Middle Ages it was scarcely considered in itself, and the Church justified those points of doctrine, and especially of liturgy and discipline, that she considered obligatory and that lacked explicit scriptural foundation, by a fairly vague appeal to unwritten traditions and above all by an appeal to her own authority, given by God and assisted by his Spirit. The whole of this was known as *traditiones*. In order to counter more effectively what they considered an abuse of the Church's authority, the Reformers rejected everything indiscriminately, regarding these unscriptural additions as "purely human traditions". Against the Reformers, the Council of Trent merely insisted on the existence and value of *apostolic* traditions, without dealing precisely and extensively with the problem of *the* tradition.

Protestants today readily agree that the sixteenth-century Reformers neither dealt with nor were even aware of the real problem of tradition. And in addition, circumstances having changed, they themselves are showing an interest not only in this problem, but also in that of traditions. In their ecumenical meetings they have received proof of their existence. Gathered around the Bible and united by it, the representatives of different Protestant churches at their ecumenical meetings have admitted the evidence of an elementary experience. An Orthodox delegate at the Edinburgh Conference of August 1937, Professor Hamilcar Alivisatos, confessed that "he had never realized the force and influence of a tradition, even though his own Orthodox tradition went back to the origins of Christianity, before meeting his brothers of the Reformed churches and seeing the tenacity with which they defended traditions which, compared with his own, were, however, very recent." Pastor J.-D. Benoît, who quoted this example, added: "In fact this concerns us too; we are all dependent on our traditions much more than we imagine." [5] Statements of this kind are so numerous today that a dozen others could be quoted.

In the same ecumenical climate Protestants also understand more fully the extent to which they depend on a historical continuity, a fact previously overlooked, if not actually denied, by them. O. Cullmann wrote in 1953: "We, on the Protestant side, are beginning to understand the immense

[5] J.-D. Benoît, "Impressions d'un délégué", *Le Christianisme social* (Sept.–Oct., 1937): 279.

wealth that is contained in the writing of the Church Fathers and are beginning to rid ourselves of the strange conception of the Church's history that claims that, with the exception of a few sects, there was a total eclipse of the Gospel between the second and sixteenth centuries." [6]

This rediscovery of the existence of a historical continuity, combined with the renewal of interest in dogma and with the profound attention paid to the Church as a reality, has resulted in an intellectual comprehension that Christianity lives basically on the principle of tradition, in the profound sense of the word, that is, of the transmission through space and time of a deposit laid down once and for all.

This accounts for the creation of a commission to study the question of tradition, in the ecumenical movement within the framework of the World Council of Churches. Adopted at the Conference of Lund in August 1952, the project led to the creation in 1954 of a commission comprising a section in Europe and one in the United States with the task of studying "tradition and traditions". Here "traditions" are taken to mean the concrete forms of Christianity found in the different confessions because they have been *received*: they are of a human, historical and sociological character. Each Church lives concretely within and according to certain traditions. By "tradition" is understood that which underlies all this: the reality of God's gift to the world, of Jesus Christ "delivered unto us"—in short, Christianity and the essentials of the Christian message. This tradition possesses a normative value.

The studies resulting from this research or carried out simultaneously on a personal basis have shown unmistakable signs

[6] *Cahiers théols*, vol. 33, *La Tradition: Problème exégétique, historique et théologique* (Neuchâtel and Paris, 1953), p. 53.

of progress.[7] A first assessment may be attempted following the Fourth World Conference of Faith and Constitution, held in Montreal in July 1963. It is already clear that, if on the Protestant side there has been a frank and positive appraisal of the situation, the progress toward agreement already begun is meeting with considerable obstacles. To begin with, not everyone would agree with O. Cullmann about the value he is prepared to recognize in the events of the Church's history. And Cullmann himself, having recognized the value of tradition, stops short when it is a question of accepting it as a norm. The tradition of *the apostles* alone has this quality; and he states that we can reach this tradition with certainty, today, only in and by their writings. It is possible that he considers this tradition in a way that is too exclusively intellectual, a mistake that has been made equally by many Catholic apologists since the sixteenth century, regarding it as an immediate means of increasing our knowledge; whereas there exists an apostolic tradition forming an integral part, as it were, either of the Church's general dogmatic position, which governs an interpretation of the Bible that has been largely retained by the Reformers themselves, or of the liturgy and Christian customs, which they have wrongly despised and rejected. In any case, the questions concerning tradition that still separate the Protestants from us all lead to the problem of ecclesiology. There is no escaping it. Indeed, the basic question is this: Has tradition an *autonomous* value, albeit subordinated to that of Scripture, or does its entire value come from Scripture, which it interprets?

[7] In chapter 7 of *La Tradition et les traditions*, vol. 2, *Essai théologique* (Fayard, 1963), which is long and heavily documented, I have attempted to present, if not an assessment, at least a critical account of the progress achieved during the last decade: results, suggestions and basic questions that need exploring more fully.

The Catholic reply is that tradition represents a value in its own right, apart from Scripture, a value that becomes a norm. This reply supposes the recognition of another gift, other than Scripture, made to men by God to unite them to him in a holy fellowship. This gift is that of the ecclesiastical institution and of the Holy Spirit, who dwells within it and guides it. But this raises the whole question of the religious relationship, of the divine institution of an assorted ministry of powers and gifts, and finally of the nature of the Church as the Body of Christ. It is at this level that research and a confrontation of ideas seem necessary in order to make any headway toward agreement on a question that has been debated for more than four centuries and that could perhaps be stated more clearly.

In the meantime the Catholic Church herself is not hardening her position. More than one of the theologians quoted in this book, or in my two-volume *Essai*, have made useful contributions to disengage these positions from the mass of developments resulting from the controversy. A consensus of opinion seems to have been established among us, which may be summed up as follows: it is impossible to deny the existence of truths belonging to the revealed deposit without being formally attested in Scripture. And yet the latter presents the whole Christian mystery. The role of tradition, from a dogmatic point of view, is to communicate its authentic interpretation, the substance of which was transmitted from the beginning and has been rendered progressively explicit by the reflection of the Doctors and the action of the Magisterium, especially in the great Ecumenical Councils. If it is considered in its totality, equally as tradition and traditions, its role is also educative and conservative with regard to the "Catholic spirit". By all these means, tradition gives the *whole* Gospel, developed by the mind of the Church throughout the ages and illuminated by her experience of the realities of which it speaks, ever present within her to nourish her life; similarly Scripture gives the *whole* Gospel regarding the essentials of the Christian mystery, of which it speaks throughout. Both are complete, but tradition renders explicit things that Scripture contains merely in principle: such things, for example, as the scriptural canon, the canon of the sacraments, and many points not only in Marian theology but in "theology" in general, such as the personal divinity of the Holy Spirit or the equality of the divine Persons.

Both Scripture and tradition are necessary to arrive at a full knowledge of the saving deposit; they are two means by which the latter reaches us. However, the expression "two sources" should be avoided because it demands subtle explanations and would risk confining the theology of tradition within a debatable position precisely whose narrowness we are trying to overcome.

As is known, the expression "two sources of Revelation" was rejected by a near two-thirds majority at the Second Vatican Council. This decision is of considerable importance for the future of the dialogue on this question between the Protestants and ourselves. As a well-informed commentator noted on this subject: "With this vote of November 20th (1962), it may be said that the period of the Counter-Reformation is at an end, and that Christianity is entering a new era whose consequences are as yet unpredictable." [8]

---

[8] R. Rouquette, "Bilan du Concile", *Études* (January 1963): 104.

SELECT BIBLIOGRAPHY

ALTANER, Berthold. *Patrology*. New York: Herder and Herder; London: Nelson, 1960.

CASSIDY, F. P. *Molders of the Medieval Mind*. St. Louis: Herder, 1944.

CONGAR, Yves M. J., O.P. *Lay People in the Church*. 2d ed. London: Geoffrey Chapman; Westminster, Md.: Newman Press, 1957.

————. *Mystery of the Church*. Baltimore: Helicon Press, 1960.

DIRKSEN, A. H. *Elementary Patrology: The Writings of the Fathers of the Church*. St. Louis: Herder, 1959.

DVORNIK, Francis. *The Ecumenical Council*. New York: Hawthorn Books, 1961.

HANSON, R. P. C. *Origen's Doctrine of Tradition*. London: S.P.C.K., 1954.

JALLAND, T. G. *The Origin and Evolution of the Christian Church*. New York: Rinehart, 1950.

JOURNET, Charles. *What Is Dogma?* Translated by Mark Pontifex. New York: Hawthorn Books, 1964.

KELLY, J. N. D. *Early Christian Creeds*. New York and London: Longmans, 1950.

KIDD, B. J. *Documents Illustrative of the Christian Church*. London: S.P.C.K., 1938.

KNIGHT, G. A. F. *Biblical Theology of the Old Testament*. Richmond, Va.: John Knox Press, 1959.

LABRIOLLE, Pierre Champagne de. *History and Literature of Christianity from Tertullian to Boethius*. New York: Knopf, 1925.

LUBAC, Henri de, S.J. *Catholicism: Christ and the Common Destiny of Man*. Translated by Lancelot C. Sheppard and Sister Elizabeth Englund, O.C.D. San Francisco: Ignatius Press, 1998.

NEWMAN, J. H. *An Essay on the Development of Doctrine*. London: Longmans, several eds. from 1846; New York: Doubleday, Image Books, 1959.

QUASTEN, J. *Patrology*. Vols. 1 and 2. Westminster, Md.: Newman Press, 1950 and 1953.

RÉTIF, André, S.J. *The Catholic Spirit*. New York: Hawthorn Books, 1959.

TAVARD, George H. *Holy Writ or Holy Church: The Crisis of the Protestant Reformation*. London: Burns and Oates; New York: Harper, 1959.